# TONGUES

# MICHEAL O'SIADHAIL

# TONGUES

BLODAXE BOOKS

ISBN: 978 1 85224 874 1

First published 2010 by
Bloodaxe Books Ltd,
Highgreen,
Tarset,
Northumberland NE48 1RP.

**www.bloodaxebooks.com**
For further information about Bloodaxe titles
please visit our website or write to
the above address for a catalogue.

 Supported by
**ARTS COUNCIL
ENGLAND**

Cover design: Neil Astley & Pamela Robertson-Pearce.

Printed in Great Britain by
Bell & Bain Limited, Glasgow, Scotland.

*For Eileen Hallinan, Hallgrímur Magnússon, Chie Nakamura and all who nurtured me in tongues.*

# ACKNOWLEDGEMENTS

Acknowledgments are due to the editors of the following publications, in which some of these poems first appeared *The Irish Book Review*, *David Jones Society Journal*, *Burren Villages: Tales of History and Imagination* (Mercier Press, 2010), *Auguri: To Mary Kelleher* (Royal Dublin Society, 2009) and *Honouring the Word: Poetry and Prose Celebrating Maurice Harmon's 80th Birthday* (Salmon Poetry, 2010).

# CONTENTS

## GRAMMAR

## UNDER THE SIGN

## GRATITUDE

# FOREWORD

Isn't language an extraordinary thing? And to think that everyone has a language! It's such a take-for-granted part of all our daily lives and everything we do. It's the most distinctive human gift. Not only do we all learn and know a language but a large majority of people as mothers and fathers know the joy of being language teachers, the delight of passing on their own mother tongue.

What is also amazing is how average four-year-olds, without ever being specifically taught complex rules, can not only speak grammatically but can come up with sentences they have never heard before. It seems that we have an innate facility to acquire language. There is good linguistic and even genetic evidence, that we're hardwired to work language.

Yet we never finish and never completely know even our own language. We go on learning all our lives. If we enter a trade or profession we learn the jargon. Someone uses a phrase you never heard before and you pick it up. Think of all the new words my generation absorbed in the technological revolution we're living through as we entered a new world of 'booting up', 'dropdown menus', 'taskbars' and 'spam filters'. If you take up a new sport there are 'genoas' or 'birdies'. Part of children's fascination with Tolkien's *Lord of the Rings* is the variety of languages he invents for the Middle-Earth. Any new cult or subculture we enter will teach us a whole new vocabulary whether it's the criminal underworld of 'fencing' or the 'consciousness raising' of a political subgroup. We're endless language learners.

And words are so strange. Each seems to have an aura of its own. Whole institutions split over a word. The Roman Catholic Church and the Eastern Orthodox Church parted from about 1054 over the addition of *filioque* (and the Son) to the Nicene Creed. People kill one another over words. Think of the use of 'ethnic cleansing' in Eastern Europe or how in the Rwandan genocide the Hutu branded the Tutsi as 'cockroaches'.

There are whole fields and networks of meaning. Over time meanings slide and change. When I was a boy 'adult' only meant 'grown-up'. Then it was used to convey 'suitable for adults'. Now it also means 'pornographic' as in an 'adult movie'. We're half-conscious of the transition. The shifts of sense and usage accumulate over hundreds even thousands of years within one language.

Then again languages are related. Even a quick glance at the word for 'mother' in, say, Spanish and Italian *madre*, Catalan *mare*, French *mère* and Portuguese *mãe* would lead you think that there was something in common. On balance if we compare these various words for 'mother', we might work out what they have in common and build up a picture of what word they might all be derived from. In fact, we know that historically all of them were originally Latin and so they all come from Latin *mater*. But there again if we take a wider angle and look at the word for 'mother' in, for example, Latin *mater*, English *mother*, Irish *máthair*, Greek *mētēr* and *mātár-* in the language of ancient India, by using the same comparative method, we might work out what word they should all have come from. Given the variations we'd reckon on a word like *mātér* as its origin. Here we don't know the history but we have to believe that in all probability this language existed. This hypothetical common ancestral language must have spread across most parts of Europe and in certain parts of India.

Scholars making use of the comparative method and what they call 'internal reconstruction', that is working out the original form within a group of closely related languages, have figured out with an extraordinary degree of precision not only the words but also the grammar of this hypothetical language, which they call 'Proto-Indo-European'. On top of this, we can get some picture of the culture, the society and environment, the economy and technology, even the religion and poetics of those who spoke this language. There is a lot of controversy as to exactly when and where this language was spoken. It's largely agreed that it probably had split into differing dialects by the third millennium BC.

While in an example like 'mother' it is relatively easy to see the relationship, this is not always so. The nexus of rules describing the developments and connections are so well worked through that words which, on the surface seem most unlikely to be related are revealed to have a common origin. For instance, at first there seems little connection between English 'queen', the Irish word *bean* meaning woman (which has entered English as the first element in 'banshee') and the Greek word *gunē*, 'woman' (which we see in the first part of 'gynecology').

Of course there are many other large families of languages besides the Indo-European. There are Sino-Tibetan, Semitic, Ural-Altaic families and so on. Some have tried to find common origins for a number of these families, but this is highly speculative.

Why am I explaining all this? I just want to give a sense of the scope of the shifts and linkages. In meditating on words, I want to allow these relationships shine through and illuminate the intricate marvel of language.

As a poet I'm utterly intrigued by the rampant imagination of human beings. I think of Wallace Stevens's famous 'Thirteen Ways of Looking at a Blackbird'. Languages have infinite ways of looking at one thing. In English there is the 'presentation' of a prize. It has all the resonances of present or gift and has its origin in the Latin for something which 'is before' someone. That seems to a speaker of English straightforward enough. But then in French it's a 'delivery' or 'handing over' (*remise*), in German it's 'hiring out' or 'loaning' (*Verleihung*), in Icelandic 'a parting with or handing over' (*afhenda*) and so on. Again to an English speaker it's clear that you can wear hats, shirts, trousers, gloves or glasses, while in Japanese there is a different verb used for all of these. Or to take the example of an idiom in English, it rains 'cats and dogs' but in French it's 'strings' (*de cordes*), in Irish 'a cobler's knives' (*sceanna gréasaí*) and in Welsh 'old women and sticks' (*hen wragedd a fyn*). There's just four ways of looking at rain. But of course it's endless.

The great linguist Edward Sapir once said 'every language itself is a collective art of expression... An artist may utilise the aesthetic resources of his speech. He may be thankful if the given palette of colours is rich, if the springboard is light. But he deserves no special credit for felicities which are the language's own.' For a while in the first half of the 20th century, Sapir and another linguist Benjamin Whorf propounded the view that the language a person speaks affects the way that he or she thinks, meaning that the structure of the language itself affects cognition. The standard example was the number of words (later shown to be somewhat exaggerated) Eskimos have for snow. This view, though no doubt it has some validity, is too deterministic.

Life is more porous and clearly we can acquire other languages.

This brings me to that unbelievable joy of learning a new language. There is a special delight in discovering how things can be said differently. The feeling of becoming a child again and being the butt of everybody else's knowledge. Yet being an adult you're able to be guided by a tradition of grammar and rules. You're trying to get your tongue and head to chime. There is a rollercoaster of feelings of elation and despair, of progress and shortfall. Sometimes there's a sense of *déjà entendu* as if some latent part of your personality is waking. And you're not just learning words but also a history, a geography, an entire culture. Then a whole new world of friendships is growing.

I mentioned the word grammar. This is in some ways an astounding phenomenon. We have here the basic patterns on which we can turn endless variations. It's a way of keeping the 'ecology' of the personal innovation and the possibility of community in play. It's the genetic code that allows for infinite mutations. Or to put it another way, it's the tune on which we can riff to our heart's content.

For many children of my generation the word conjures up hours of parsing and analysis and learning declensions and conjugations off by heart. I began Latin at primary school where we learned our verbs off by heart as we learned our tables. *Amo, amas, amat.* But looking back on the wealth of terms we used – 'the ablative absolute', 'the prolative infinitive', 'the sequences of tenses' and 'final clauses' – I'm amazed at how as children we just drank in these mysterious expressions. I wasn't surprised when I discovered years later that the word 'glamour' was originally 'grammar'. It was apparently a Scottish variant of the word 'grammar', which because it was associated with learning came to mean 'magic'. And so the meanings 'charm', 'allure', 'excitement', though often with a connotation of the ephemeral. But little did I as a schoolboy think... I want now to return, to make these terms my own, to enjoy the strange enchantment: *'verbs of hoping, promising, threatening, swearing are usually followed by the future infinitive...'*

Some years ago when my books started to appear in Japanese translation, with the help of my translator and friend, Professor Shigeo Shimizu, I started to try to tackle Japanese.

I became fascinated by those fantastic 'characters' or signs. You know the way you've so often seen what seems just a blur of eastern squiggles on a restaurant or shop front but you couldn't for the life of you distinguish one from the other, not to mention remembering them or imagine how they could convey meaning. It began to dawn on me that we use such signs here in Europe too. We all know how a stylised figure of a man or woman signs which toilet we head for. Or how a knife and fork sign in a list of hotels tells us there is a restaurant. Again a stylised figure in a wheelchair indicates facilities for the disabled. But what may at first appear to us as squiggles is a whole system of such signs that has evolved over something like four millennia and which can be read by about a sixth of the world's population. But what grabs me is that these 'characters' can express all abstract thought. One thing is to draw some picture of a concrete object but how do you illustrate concepts like 'worry', 'meaning', 'experience'?

These signs or characters derive from ones which originated between 2000 and 1500 BC in the Yellow River region of China. The earliest were inscribed on bones and tortoise shells. Starting as simple they grew abstract, complex and highly stylised. They were brought to Japan by Chinese and Korean migrants about the third or fourth century AD. In Japanese, these signs can be read as Chinese loan-words or as native Japanese words. For example 言 can be read as *gen* if taken as a Chinese borrowed word or as *koto* if read as the native Japanese word.

Normally the Japanese are only conscious of the origin of the most transparent characters. Otherwise they are largely unaware, just as English speakers don't know the roots of most words they use daily. I'm by no means the first western poet to meditate on these signs. Probably the most famous example in English is Ezra Pound's *Cantos*. He had been introduced to them through Ernest Fenollosa's work. Fenollosa spent long periods in Japan and contributed greatly to Japanese culture. At one point he travelled through America with a magic lantern lecturing on these signs. The *Cantos* were written between about 1915 and 1956. But there is also the earlier French-language tradition with figures such as the Belgian Henri Michaux and later, such works as Paul Claudel's *Connaissance de l'Est* (1900) and Victor Segalen's *Stèles* (1912).

And yet we've gone beyond any simple 'Orientalia' and in a culture bombarded by visual images, these signs remain rich enough to sustain endless meditations.

We live in a new oral and visual culture. Alongside the image comes the soundbite. In any language, proverbs are a source of metaphor and wisdom. When someone says 'there is no smoke without fire', nobody looks around to find a fire. It's like the third line of a haiku and we know at once this isn't to be taken literally. It sums up the long hard-earned experience of a community and saves it reinventing the wheel over and over again.

I find the variation in metaphors from language to language quite astonishing. Sometimes images must have spread from country to country. Other times the same image arose from a similar way of life, even though there probably was no contact. I love the nugget-like intensity of the proverbs; it's almost as if there was an economy of truth which is like gnomic Edda verse.

Then too there's always been a secondary, often facetious and formulaic layer of 'Wellerism' about in many languages. A Norwegian example is: Make haste slowly, said the farmer as he ate his porridge with an awl. I believe cynical proverbs were popular in Soviet Russia. Perhaps there is some connection between the level of public trust and the frequency of these undercuttings of traditional wisdom. And they go on showing up in new circumstance or to turn an old fashioned sentiment upside down. Popular in Norway among women, for instance: 'when God created the human being, she began with a rough draft' or 'men will be men, strong and childish'.

Of course, the suspicion of language itself has been at the heart of many intellectual quandaries. Interwoven with Marxist, feminist and postcolonial critiques, language itself has been doubted. Jacques Derrida and Michel Foucault played with the Saussurean view of the sign as an arbitrary convention. Roland Barthes argued that the sign had to be seen as a sign in order not to underpin illusions of reality. Paul de Man went a stage further insisting that language is always weaving between the literal and the metaphorical which in the end renders it unreadable. And so on...

This line of suspicion largely derives from Ferdinand de Saussure's view of language as a complete system of signs.

On the other hand the French philosopher Paul Ricœur has opened up again the whole question of the relation of the sign to reality and imagination. Clearly there is no one-to-one linkage but rather a complex interaction. Language is vital for history's narrative or for a judge's decision or for great works of fiction. According to Ricoeur 'through the capacity of language to create and recreate, we discover reality itself in the process of being re-created...language in the making creates reality in the making'. Our sense of who we are is mediated through language.

In the end I know all the dangers and suspicion and yet I must trust. Only by keeping the whole scope and richness of words and signs in play, by feasting on the fullness of language can we hope to allow this our unique human gift to flourish.

My friend the painter Mick O'Dea once told me how he has all his life been enthralled by paint, by the feeling of taking clay and the oils of the earth and daubing them on a canvas. As a poet I know nothing quite like the thrill of taking these organised sounds and signs we make and shaping them in sequences of rhythm and meaning. I want to hold up the wonder of tongues and say: How about this?

# WONDER

*Men hugse det bør vi:*
*Eit ord er eit under.*

Yet remember we ought
A word is a wonder.

TOR JONSSON

# A Basin in a Kyōto Temple Garden

## 1

Built just before Byzantium fell
In Ryōanji's stone and moss garden
The *tsukubai* or 'crouching basin',

A vice-Shōgun's gift with its ladle
Waiting for a monk who'll bow and bale
A scoop of water to cleanse his soul

And ponder the Zen of these four signs:
Above a 5, a bird to the right,
Below a foot, leftside an arrow.

## 2

吾 唯 足 知
*Ware tada taru o shiru*
I only know contentment

Can humankind bear
Very much reality?
All that might have been.
Burnt Norton's five commands
Echo down this garden.
*Go, go, go* said Eliot's bird,
*Quick, find them, find them*
Lost footprints of shaven monks
Time's arrow forgets
In basins of squared silence,
But scoop now deeper
This whole greater than its parts:
The pool too a sign,
With 5, bird, foot and arrow.
Clockwise these symbols read
*I only know contentment.*

3

Contentment? What am I doing here
At Eurasia's opposite end
A pilgrim on another island?
*Iyashii* 'lowly' their adjective,
*The contented both rich and humble,*
A bottomless well of contentment
Cupped up in a small bamboo ladle.
A Zenic moment. A lavishment.
But dippers stir a storm in ripples,
And there in the shimmering water
Once more I face my Madam Desire.


4

For the umpteenth time
To shed an easy-peasy
Native tongue, become
A player in other plays.
I reincarnate
A child soaking every word.
A strange *déjà vu*
Awakes an oriental self.
Born again, remothered me.


5

No Byzantium I sail to.
Glittering light, a cloud that passes
Caught in waters of reality,
Contentment always in the doing.
Five symbols and one to share with four
To keep both the whole and parts in play.
Did I ever choose to see that face?
O lifelong cupidinous arrow,
Footfall memory of what might have been,
O bird of desire still haunting me.

# Rebirths

Thrill of such rebirths,
Pangs of growing to
Other take-for-grantedness

Until I forget
Any time before,
As though this was always me.

A favourite song,
Aroma of foods,
Jokes about neighbour countries.

Webs of reference,
When to thank or bow,
The meaning of a friend's name.

Babel's giddy world:
Once masks, now faces,
New ways I see and am seen.

Have I stepped outside
An innocent ring,
My garden never the same?

Still no turning back.
All houses now tents
A nomadic mind has pitched:

Finnegans Waker,
The only reader,
*The perfect insomniac.*

No complete sharer.
Polyglot loneness.
Rich creole of memories.

# Unless

### 1

Unless you behave
As little children
These kingdoms too shut their gates.
After the first rush,
Kiss of new vowels,
Strange sound used and understood,
Again your childhood
Hangs on others' words.
Rollercoaster of regrowth:
That Japanese man
Blunderingly called
A widower to his face;
Misunderstandings
All my humbling *faux pas*,
Yokes of initiation,
Words over your head,
A whispered put-down,
Butt of everyone's knowing.
Feelings of despair
As progress plateaus –
What's the point in bothering?
Temptations to yield.
Never fully there.
Still a sense of belonging.
A world glimpsed I can't give up.

### 2

Unless venturing
A shy child within
No one dares to mother me.
An adult guard down,
Weakness my defence,
First move in a love affair.
New friends' protégé,
A grateful pupil,
Nurtured beyond my nature
I'm finding my tongue.

And begin to shape
Yet another persona.
Slowly I absorb,
Psyche tuning in
Like a diplomat returned
From too long abroad,
Stretching to adopt
Other angles of vision.
Lifelong induction –
Still an apprentice
I resound parent voices.
Echoing their gift,
In their light I learn
First to creep and then to walk,
Hold my own among the tribe.

# Overlap

A hidden image lurks behind each word,
Some secret cargo stored below my mind,
A resonance, a coloured first-time heard,
Recalled frisson never quite defined.
And still each word remains a public tool,
Enough shared sense to manage all we mean,
Unconscious mix of anarchy and rule,
A subtle compromise, a go-between.
Associations half tied-down, half free,
A zone at once both on and off the map,
All history and story interwound
In straddled borderlands of 'us' and 'me'
Where memories and kinship overlap –
Our inner echo room, our common ground.

# Undertones

### 1

Please don't say the word 'highly-strung'.
My childhood wakes again in me.
What did whispering adults mean?

Whatever they were murmuring
Part for me, part behind my back,
Was it my fault, something I said?

Amata? Stradivarius?
The pegs tautening creakingly
Over my bridge and fingerboard.

Virtuoso temperament
Quavering from scroll to tailpiece,
Stick and rosined bow of passion.

Adult now, so not to my face,
But when I shed an old image,
Another dreaded adjective.

The moment I think I'm placid
Or reining in my eagerness:
*Ah, but you're so very intense!*

Violins pick up the rhythm
Pizzicatoing across the years
A sense of half-understood shame.

### 2

Well, well. What talk of violins?
'A person or an animal
Nervous and easily upset',
'Sensitive, excitable child' –
Lexicons keep our common core
But don't you hear background hum,
A charge behind the metaphor?

Perhaps it was once archery,
A D-shaped narrow-limbed longbow's
Arrow tense from nock to head,
Fletched and ready but still too taut
Before its moment of release,
A short linen fibre drawn taut,
So overstrung, so overwrought.

No, no! For me the violin.
A stick ricochets and bounces
Across the upper gut-strings pegged
Shamelessly tight. And let it be.
I can't care less. Rosin the bow.
My life played out against a pulse.
High tension of concert pitch.

# Worlds

### 1

How many words have Eskimos for snow?
Do we only see what we already know?

For some no need to split their greens and blues.
We learn to break our rainbow into hues.

Our language our conspiracies of thought,
A web of metaphors that we were taught.

That futures lie ahead just in the mind,
For Ayamara the unseen lay behind.

Enigma interplay of thought and word
The lines of shape and shaper always blurred.

### 2

Die. They die and die.
Hundreds on our globe,
Waning to a last speaker.

All five continents,
Ainu to Zazao,
A to Z of dwindlings.

Lost in children's play.
Mothers who don't dare.
Languages move up the line.

Tongues fall to silence
Their worlds unravelling
Broken threads of might have been.

### 3

Once an Araner's lost blank stare.
In Dublin the ward nurses declare

Him deaf. He can't understand.
Once only he'd been on mainland.

Message clear (intended or not):
A world unsafe for a monoglot.

So fast our futures slip behind.
His image refuses to quit my mind.

Again the Ainu face in Kyōto,
The gaze of a Canadian Eskimo.

All standing still our slow downfall.
This flux and change I can't forestall.

# Turnstile

'Adult and a chiseller,' father said
And I made myself as small as I could
When he pushed me ahead through the turnstile
Pleased with himself that he'd saved a tanner.

'I did, faith,' I imagine him claiming
Or 'Don't you bother about that, brother!'
Layers of language somehow glide from me
Like those years of quid and bob and copper.

Each generation's gradual slippage,
Ephemeral poetry of slang,
Idioms, patterns, soft shifts of meaning –
The day Middle English slipped to modern.

What is it in me that can't quite manage
That confident intransitive: *Enjoy!*
Or saying *cool* or how at last *I'd gotten*
*To* try out another *medication*?

No, this is life. I take it as it is.
Even such strange returns of older forms.
It's just I know my age. I bow my head
As the turnstile's bar clicks against my chest.

# Grooves

### 1

Millennia hide behind each utterance
A silted mind below a shimmering pool,
Each tongue's conspiracy a matrix of nuance
In unremembered change and shifts of rule.
Such worlds of connotations left unsaid,
Our slang and jargon plots inside a plot;
So many depths, so many circles spread,
Within our own are we a polyglot?
Our voice a sound dispersed in time and tense,
Unconscious breath in any act of speech
Sending through its hum and plosion daughter
Dispatches, subtle overtones of sense,
Unfolding rings, circuitries of outreach,
Our every word a pebble dropped in water.

### 2

Smack and kiss of lips that spread around,
Feel of tongue shaping flows of air
Knowing how to streamline any sound,
Curl and arch of oral savoir-faire.
Sheer delight before the paradigm,
Buzz of groove and tooth with z between,
Jabberwocky thrill of nonsense rhyme,
Taste of words before the thing they mean.
Vowels ooze around my chortling tongue
Finding whatever curve they need to voice
Liquid music's humming jubjub bird;
Vocal chords a violin highly-strung
Freighting through my mouth a dancing voice,
Endless joy of one incarnate word.

### 3

My life of rubbings-off and overlays –
The way we gather from those we chance to meet
From day to day some word or maybe phrase
I've heard and half-unknowingly repeat.
However much an island, however clannish,

Our language too an archaeology –
For us the Latin, Vikings and Spanish –
It's Dutch or Portuguese through Nagasaki.
No archipelago to own outright,
We touch on hidden continental shelves;
No insulation, nothing's watertight,
We are such shifting laminated selves.
In any dream whatever rules we flout,
Each word a gene in stories we print out.


4

What unknown was first to coin a word,
Single imaginations breaking through,
Strings of sounds that no one before had heard
Someone dared to find and make it new.
Hoarded combinations still untried,
Meanings so rich and manifold,
Keeping within the metaphors they hide
Endless elbowroom inside the mould.
Prod and pull of untold slide and change
Editing a culture's omnibus,
Long communal art, experience wrought
Over years of drift and need to rearrange,
Generations shaping and reshaping us,
Ages carving out our grooves of thought.


5

Of course the easy groove of how I came.
Perhaps my cast of mind, a temperament
That opened up between the self and same
So I delight in all that's different.
Such once-offness, unique modes of speech
And yet the analogues I can't ignore
In spite of meanings overlaps and breach,
For all our unlike names one human core?
If only how we learn to analyse,
As children grasping grammars unaware,
Or even ways as adults we zigzagwise
Could find with time the door to anywhere.
Whatever universals allow us move;
My transit lives still slide from groove to groove.

# Kyōto by Night

Night on endless night a Kyōto hotel
narrows its room around my sleeplessness
playing back a lifetime in my skull.

I'd read the door and all the bathroom signs,
proud of my *kanji*, found how the window worked,
whiled an hour with a local radio broadcast.

Tonight at wits' end the resident masseuse
plump and skilled tackles me part by part:
*Fukurahagi* she names my tensed up calves.

One of eight from Kyūshū, grandparent now,
each evening a half an hour by motorbike
for four sessions with her hotel clientele.

Her husband when he's drunk still beats her –
*pon pon!* she illustrates with her clenched fists –
*bon no kubo*, she presses the nape of my neck.

Twice a year back to her childhood island:
Lantern Festival or visits to her parents' grave.
'Too busy here,' she tells my impatient head.

Soon she'll home for a beer or two and bed.
Her story fills a sterile room with warmth.
I'm grateful and glad I came so far to listen.

Her thumbs print my brainstems with ease;
the press of *anma* elbowing into my mind,
I tumble towards an ecstasy of sleep.

Satō-san? Nakamura-san? Suzuki-san?
Have I forgotten to ask my kneader's name?
My anonymous grandmother is biking into the night.

# WORD

How long a time lies in one little word!

WILLIAM SHAKESPEARE: *Richard II*

# Lullaby

Stains are in, stains are in,
The instant our songs begin

To rockabye my darling baby
Dreaming up worlds of maybe.

Then *byssa, byssa barnet*
Beddie byes my snowy Arne,

Quieter now and slumber-bound,
Rest in lulls of milky sound.

*Ninna nanna, ninna nanna,*
*La mia bambina italiana.*

*Aja papaya, aja papaja*
Doze so *meine kleine Freya.*

Hushabye and *nen-nen-yo*
The moon is high in Tokyo.

*Bí bí og blaka* Viking Anna,
*Seoithín, seoithín, seó a leanbh,*

All is well I wouldn't lie,
Trust again this bye and bye.

Valleys deep and dark unruly,
Dafydd Bach, *si hei lwli.*

*Kuus, kuus, kalike,*
My Tallinn child night won't stay.

Sandman fallen, lullaby sung,
Sleep my love in a mother tongue.

# Mother

Whenever I think of snow I think of her.
Barely a dozen days after she bore me
It began. Forty-seven and over a smother

Of soggy turf she folds a relentless nappy.
Summer the wettest in decades. Still rations:
Two ounces of butter, half an ounce of tea,

Half pound of sugar a week, six of bread.
A big post-war radio forecast crackles
Six weeks of blizzards and drifts ahead.

*Mère, madre, mare, maire* or *madro*
How we'd guess that *mater* was the source
But since all come from Latin know it's so.

Greek, Germanic, Celtic, Baltic, Indian
*Mater*, mother, *máthair, māte, matar:*
A theory's *māter* we call Indo-European.

Baby-talk mā, our universal feeding cry,
With *–ter*, one of two, a kinship ending.
Hoagy Carmichael sings *Ole Buttermilk Sky*

In the clothed speaker of an Atwater Kent,
Its orange-dialled cabinet a hive of valves
And condensers someone in America sent.

First son, soon apple of her longing eye.
Thirty-five and matrix of castles in the air.
A flurry of dreams curdles the January sky.

## Snows

Here a two-hour train-ride north of Oslo
Leaden November flurries usher in
Six insisting months of snow –
*Sneachta, snø, nifa, sneg* or *nix* –
Swirls and wafts across
Freakish days before it layers and sticks.
Winter's falling over Raufoss.

How I love this sifting time when sap
Sinks to lull the noiseless branches down
Endless dreams that now unmap
Lines and colours autumn took for real.
Nights are ten below.
Stains of rowanberries' blood congeal,
Flaming the early snow.

Snow. Our Indo-European word,
Sniff and snivel noun of crystal flakes,
Sneaking manna blizzard,
Soundless whirlings over our cradle place.
*Sneg* and *sneachta*. Snow.
All our versions worlds that we retrace
Five thousand years ago.

Yet the need to say exactly where
Hazards lay, describe terrain or how
Best to be aware
Whether it could thaw or maybe slide,
Things a local knows,
Skills passed on or maybe pride,
Sheer delight in naming snows.

*Fonn* for drift and *gadd* for hardened snow.
Millennia and northern Europeans
Like the Eskimo
Learn to label tiers and densities.
Fluffy, soft as floss,
Crusting now as layers begin to freeze.
Winter's falling over Raufoss.

# Raufoss

*Foss* for 'falls' and *raud* for 'red',
Rapids hued by iron ore,
Traces in a river-bed.

*Eas Ruaidh* near Ballyshannon,
Red Falls in New York State,
*Cascade Rouge* in Lebanon.

*Rufus, ruds, ruadh, rot,*
Longish looping waves of light's
Five thousand years to connote

Leakings from a fountainhead
Into shoots and cataracts,
Rusted veins of minerals bled,

Vehemence of love or blood,
Rouge of cheeks and rowan lips,
Stains of passion understood,

Heartbeats raised, a blaze of fire,
Crimson sign of risk or thrill,
Sudden Niagaras of desire

Colouring this waterway.
Red-lettered tints of fêtes
Leach the falls of everyday.

# Time and Tide

Falling through an hourglass waist
Our sifts of time and tide;
The root of both nouns a verb 'to divide'.

Our moments that drop grain by grain
Before the pendulum lock,
Before the shivering quartz or caesium clock.

Days under the sun, nights moon-paced
And measured in ebb and flow,
Gravities of spring or neap, an undertow

In rhythm's rise and cadence. *Tid* for a Dane
Is 'time', like Yuletide,
While *time* is 'hour'. Slowly words glide

On scales of subtlety. In the Italian *tempo*
Or Gaelic *aimsir* together
In one word the sense of 'time' and 'weather'.

Tides and seasons shifting to and fro.
Drifts of thought that grew,
Palette of meaning shaded hue by hue.

# Hues

A dancing light, a surface's reflection
Pigment and douse the brain with shafts of colour,
As waves and rays reveal
Hues of a spectrum's schism,
Brilliance diffused in nature's showcase

Delighting in frequencies of perfection,
Green and yellow peppers, arrays of colour,
Black skirts, a red sail,
The rainbow's liquid prism,
Joseph's coat in the common place.

How Irish and Japanese switch direction:
Our *dathúil* 'handsome' derives from colour
*Iro* can mean sex appeal,
Colour and eroticism
Blur this one semantic space.

I puzzled a while over this connection,
A drift along a scale of meaning from colour
To allure, a peacock's tail,
A shift of sense, a bowdlerism
In reverse I couldn't trace.

But 'hue' is Swedish *hy* for complexion
And Iceland's countenance has a word for colour.
Two meanings dovetail.
Our desire's rouge and chrism,
The glows and glories of a face.

# Face

'I'll break your face for you!'
A fist knuckling the tense air,
Angry schoolboy menace

And an ugly set-to
Smouldering that seems to flare
Up in a Japanese

Phrase – *kao o tsubusu* –
Learned three dozen years later
'To crush or squash a face',

Which now has more to do
With ignominy, a slur,
Lost countenance, disgrace

Cradling shame's peekaboo
Behind fingers, bad odour,
An eastern losing face

Our Old Irish knew:
*Enech* for face or honour,
A good name we abase.

Lives such pride can undo.
East or west same brittle core.
Our schoolboy human race

Still dreams of something new,
Whatever is wanting to dare
Some vulnerable space

Where nothing can subdue
A heart grown beyond such care.
An unloseable face.

# Understanding

I imagine the face of some guest
In a strange house standing under
A roof studying the ties and beams
To understand a new design.
*Ich verstehe!* Germanic
Standing against, around, under,
A fathoming of wonder.

Childhood's soaking up and in –
Nothing arm's length or standoffish –
Quiet osmosis of a gaze
As if the starer and the stared
Once merged in one amazement,
At those things we came alive to,
Awareness that fused and grew.

Yet the urge to figure out
On two islands so far apart:
The Icelandic verb *skilja*
Or the Japanese *wakaru*
Meant 'divide' or 'understand'.
Discernment. An adult mind's gift,
A grown need to screen and sift.

Our *tuigim*, a taking in,
Seizing, a coming to grips with,
Perceive, to grasp thoroughly.
So often a wish to possess.
*Je comprends!* – comprehensive
Catching on, even clinging to.
*Capito!* Now I get you!

Again Scandinavian
*Skjønne* with roots in words 'to view'.
Ageing I gaze and let go.
No need to hold or analyse.
Circles close. Enough to see.
A guest looking to understand.
A return to wonderland.

# Triad

### *Guest*

Guest had meant the one
Who stood for common
Pledges of obligation.

*Hostis* for alien,
Same word in Latin –
Double-edged non-citizen

Shuttling to and fro,
Inside outsider
Comes bit by bit to mean 'foe',

Why invite danger,
Guest or enemy,
The ambivalent stranger?

### *Host*

Host once a compound:
Guest-potentate,
Lord of hospitality,

Russian *gospodin*,
Word to venerate
A foreigner as 'master'.

But treacherous guests,
Judas at the fête,
Some hostile sleepless Macbeth

Betrayed a host's trust.
The face at the gate,
Once a stranger now a foe.

*Feast*

This word tapping down
Into sacred rites,
Things laid out before our gods.

Against all the odds
Again the stranger
Open to the stranger's face.

A toast and embrace
Repairing two words,
Our glasses raised, our eating

In tents of meeting,
A trust-mended pledge.
The host as guest, the guest host.

## Subjectivity

Was the whole world a feast for Japanese?
Europe's 'subjective' and 'objective' adapted
As either the view of host or guest.

A bird-eyed caller observes and leaves the rest
To the work of a busy host laying on a spread.
Together our life all of a piece.

# Work

'Work' in English dialects once meant 'pain'.
*In sorrow thou shalt bring...*
Labours of love. Pangs of childbirth.

French *travail* may be from Latin meaning
'Torture'. Travail of blows.
German *Arbeit* the Icelandic word for 'hard'.

Or Irish *saothar* 'work', 'panting', 'throes'.
The wintery European
Underscores an ardour in all our journeys.

A friend told me once that Thai *ngaan*
Means work or job
But also 'carnival', 'feast', 'party', 'festival'.

Those mangroved islands Europe didn't rob,
The rainforests that blurred
Lines between such sways of duty and delight.

Work parties in every sense of the word.
In bonds of toil or dance
Paradise sweats its stardust in our bones

Across three billion years of dreaming chance
From soup to angel clones.
We carry still our half-imagined Eden.

# Labyrinth

After Eden then the years of maze.
Ah, *how beautiful the world would be*
*If there were rules for moving in labyrinths.*
Umberto Eco, of course, I partly agree
Yet even such bewilderment I need to praise.

A journey of choices with no overview.
Norwegian *irrgang*, Japanese *meiro*
Both name labyrinth 'a road that strays'.
After the garden no one path to go.
No map here. No compass, chalk or clew.

Welsh *drysfa*, 'a thicket', 'a thorny place'
And I know how easily I took a turn
Meaning to remember where but hurried
Down a dead-end only again to learn
My slow retreat, forgotten steps I trace.

In labyrinths we only know we never know.
Völundur's saga house that could bewilder
Endless guests in winding rooms or passages,
Dædalus, the highflying labyrinth builder
Still leaves his trademark in Italian *dedalo*.

In tangles of images, my favourite maze;
More bumbling and roaming than astray
I love its hazy echoes of astonishment
At shuffles of choices labyrinths hold in play,
Warrens of turns that baffle and still amaze.

# Dead-ends

## *Blind Alley*

The roadway sealed as a sightless eye –
A likeness worked in several tongues,
*Uno vicolo cieco*, Norway's *blindvei*.

The traveller asks should I have known
To blind is the same as to dazzle
And dazzled was I blind as stone?

Or should, like Auden, this traveller ask
If he himself no longer sees
The light in which he loved to bask?

## *Strupcelš*

In Riga *strupcelš* means a road that's brief.
A wrong exit taken from some roundabout,

Mistaken choices, routes so badly signed
Or in reverie not quite aware how you court

Danger not watching how a road inclined
To narrow till suddenly you're pulled up short,

Another bend and there it has petered out,
An endless dream abruptly come to grief.

## 行止まり
## *Ikidomari*

In Tokyo the warning is *ikidomari*!
Two characters: a crossroads and footprint;
The one means 'go', the other 'stop dead'.

A going stop! As though someone led
You winkered up this stop-go path
Knowing there was no thoroughfare,

Knowing that this was going nowhere,
While you wove futures in your mind,
Though deeper down something in you

Sensed stalemate, an instinct that knew
What such zigzags could only mean,
You felt this road was running out.


## Cul-de-sac

Bottom of a sack! Once French for impasse,
Japan's *fukurokōji* or German *Sackgasse*.

An image to catch my first raging instinct,
Resentment at feeling somehow hoodwinked,

Trapped headlong in a bag and madly flailing
About, glimpsing the light but still just failing

To find the opening and the angrier I grow
The more I'm trapped. O irony of letting go!

The calmer, subtler easing out of a sack.
A courage gathered, the grit for turning back.


## Återvändgränd

Swedes the wisest with *återvändgränd*:
'A byway for return',
A compound noun that seems to blend

The dead-end with the turning back,
Neither denying an impasse
Or dismissing the grief in this sidetrack

And retrace to where a byroad started
To choose a different way,
Begin again where the fork had parted.

No bag or blindness, no anger or shame
In my doubling back
On roads now richer than the road you came.

So reverse here while the going is good!
*How way leads on to way –*
It might have been a New England wood.

In dead-ends at least there's no mistaking
Advance is by return,
Your journey still a journey in the making.

# Journey

Our year's journey etched on a wall –
The apex of a triangle
Inching from December's solstice
Downward allowances of sun
To flood a stone courtyard with warmth.

*Une journée*, the course of a day,
Latin for 'a daily portion',
A blending of time and motion
Which by Middle English becomes
'A day's travel', 'an excursion'.

Our journey's *per diem* of light.
The root of Latin's day is 'shine',
Likewise found in Jove or Tuesday's
Old sky-god. The way in Japanese
*Hi* can mean sun or day or light.

It's March of my sixty-first year
And an apex once too acute
Widens, obtuse and generous
Broadcasting on a courtyard wall
*Arise, shine, for thy light has come.*

A winter's granite at the core
Unchills to glint in the spring-light,
The quartzose grain of a soul
Glitters its stillness towards
A hope of warm-blooded summer.

Like Horace scaling down to now,
An ovened stone I hug this heat,
Storing every moment before
A year's angle lifts and narrows
My journey's geometries of light.

# Summer

*Fortune owns some, summer belongs to all.*
Recollected longing of evenings,
All our waiting as a new year wound up;
Half our memory our expectation,
Counting the swallows to make a summer.

And still across this northern hemisphere
Between the springing and the harvest earned
From when the sun stood still above Cancer
Until day and night again are equal,
A season's names recall the strewn traces.

Germanic 'summer' or our own *samhradh*
Showing up in Old Indian *sámā*
For 'a year' or 'a half-year' or 'season.'
If Vikings reckoned their age in winters,
Old Indians measured theirs in summers.

*Natsu* Japan's 'summer' a rambling word,
Akin or borrowed Old Turkish *jāz* 'spring',
May carry the memory of a time
When it meant 'the warmer part of the year'
And then diverged as climates demanded.

Warmth beginning our sun already turned.
A wheel moves even while it touches,
In its outset gradual retraction –
Our season arriving in its going.
Summer a word so ripe with remembrance.

# Remembrance

## *Erinnerung*

German *Erinnerung*: once 'to interiorise',
Things we've taken up, an inside story
Played again in our remembering eyes,
An archive of images, an inner repository.
Absconded moments leave their trace,
The cortex nicked, niches in our brains,
Thumbprints pressed into a wax of mind,
Whatever stamp or mark that still remains,
Our lifetimes absorbed and learnt by heart
In memories plotting back where we begin
A retrospective line across a chart,
Everything inscribed and logged within;
Etched presence of unshuttered seeing,
Indelible stains on our retina of being.

## *Ricordo*

Latin *recordatio*, act of taking
Again to heart like Japanese *kioku*
'Chronicle of thought lingering at the core'.

Cardiac high fidelity as once more
A reflexive verb snatches up a residue;
Track record of doings, inward note making.

## *Souvenir*

From Latin 'to relieve' or 'reinforce'
In the sense of 'coming up to aid',
*Subvenire* now French 'to remember'.

Hard to see how meanings can shade
Into each other and undergo
This shift from 'reinforce' to 'recall',

Unless half-consciously we know
Our stories struggle with forgetfulness,
And every souvenir a self-subvention,

*Aide-mémoire* for a stumbling psyche,
A keepsake memory we caress,
Another scratch on walls of oblivion.


## Remember

Mimir, Norse God and portal keeper,
Guard of wisdom's well,
'memory' and 'remember' double a root
We find in 'mourn'.

Latin through French 'to be again mindful'
A watchfulness grown deeper,
As all too well we know we're born
To weep and so transmute

Things past. We ward off the forgetful,
By rehearsals en route
To wisdom's gate, well worn
Paths to Mimir's well


## Reminiscence

Deliberate evocation, a thinking of.
This Indo-European men 'to mind',
Long in Irish *cuimhne*, with *'com'* combined,
In *Minnesinger* our minding turns to love.
A root that in its reminding reappears
To build again from swaps and synthesis
Renewed warmth of shared and nested stories
Unfolded out across five thousand years,
As deep within the words 'to reminisce'
We fall into step with common memories.

## *Recollect*

Recollection means a gathering up again
To find some sense among the scattered pieces,
The way we seek motives that might explain
Or more examples to prove a hunch or thesis.
We imagine both what was and will be
In the same magic lantern within a mind;
Yet in the light of slowly conjured memory
What was and now are carefully realigned.
No made-up image we might fancy or forecast
As memory for us must be a kind of work,
Checking every word against the past,
A matching truth and mind we daren't shirk.
Trusting a memory so fickle and protean,
We gather up and sift as best we can.

# Words

## *Word*

Word from an Indo-European root
'To say solemnly' or just 'to speak',
Germanic, Baltic, Greek, Latin *verbum*.

Remember school and how a verb describes
A deed or action, the way when parsing
All clauses pivoted on this doing.

Verve and charisma of an utterance,
A psychic energy in what's spoken,
Uncontainable fire in prophets' bones.

Vow, bless, threat, curse, promise or covenant,
The sway of our irrevocable sounds.
O world wanting to be taken at its word!

## *Focal*

Irish *focal* from a root 'to speak'
That comes to mean 'word' or 'noise',
Cognate with Latin *vox* for 'voice'
Or Calliope 'beautiful voice' in Greek.

Hummingbird deep in the larynx,
Words caressed on a tongue's tip
As sweet friction shivers the lip,
Our pleasure's oral high jinks.

Purr of breath still spoilt for choice
As a French kiss of a rising vowel
Shapes and flutters cheek by jowl.
I loved my muses for their voice.

# *Geir*

Welsh *geir* grounded in 'cry' or 'call'
Found in Latin for chatter, hence 'garrulous'
And turning up in Ossetian for 'nightingales'.

Or English 'care' and German *Karfreitag*
'Friday of grief' and here our cry
Itself has named the need it wails.

# 単語
# *Tango*

Mostly in the land of rising sun
Both language and word are one
But here it's *tan* 'simple' or 'single',
'one unit' of expression -*go*.

Again 'speak' and 'word' mingle:
*Go* from Chinese *yu* for speech,
Cognate with 'praise', spreads to reach
Burmese as either 'to say' or 'bird'.

What leaps of meaning occurred?
A word breaks its sound barrier
In flight. A soul's pigeon carrier
Taking wing from the word go.

# Λόγος
# *Logos*

In the fourth Gospel *logos* is the word
That was in the beginning and made flesh
With Yahweh's millennia of pledges
Echoing in one noun for 'what is said',

But laden too with Greek philosophies
Commingling with logic and -ologies,
Rules, laws, argument, reason, measure, worth,
And even for Plato bird of the soul,

Although its root had only meant 'to pluck'
Or 'gather' and then 'to read together',
'To tell', 'to speak', and so to 'the thing said'
Which in turn takes on a life of its own.

Conjure believers reading papyrus
Wondering at a prologue's parallels:
*The same was in the beginning with God.*
In a word, all and everything that is.

# Belief

### Creideamh

'Where the heart is placed'.
Irish cognate with *credo*.
Trust in core values.

### Trú

Norse, rooted in trees,
Whatever's steadfast and true.
Foliage of trust.

### 信仰　Xìnyǎng

Chinese 'trust looking up'.
Not seeing but believing.
O doubting Thomas!

### אֱמוּנָה　Emunah

Firm and secure in
Taking Moses's word as true;
Plumb-line of a world.

### Πίστις

Greek, Latin *fides* too.
Unforgetting confidence
Biding and convinced.

### Glaube

Glaube and belief
Both intensifying *leubh*:
'To care',' 'desire,' 'love'.

# Forget

## *Oblivisci*

Latin *oblivisci* 'to wipe away'
Slate rubbed clean,
An ironed-out crease.

Some half-conscious overlay,
Slip or psychic caprice
Airbrushes to oblivion.

## 忘记
## *Wàngjì*

'An account dead in the heart.'
A legend or origin tale?
Maybe. But I'm inclined

To imagine how at the start
Two Chinese lovers pined
For every trembling detail.

Then, years after they part;
Their spoors of memory fail.
O what traces die in the mind.

## *Oblidar*

Mostly we struggle with a maze
Of forgetfulness, to stay
Out of history's oubliette.

Catalan chance to reappraise
Memory's dossier.
Yes, I'm owed so much and yet...

*Oblidar*: Latin *oblitterare* 'erase',
A letter we take away.
Account closed. A cancelled debt.


## Dearmad

Like Welsh, Irish 'disremembers' –
Recalls the given state;
Forgetting a willed leaving behind.

Too easy to rake over embers.
History's bitter freight,
Hurts I wean from my mind.


## Forget

Not to apprehend –
'To lose the grip'
We try so hard to hold.

Imagine if we controlled
It all, no godsend
Of amnesia letting slip

Our blundering regret,
Like Borges's hero
Haunted by a full recall?

Give thanks for sleep's zero
When the blinds fall.
Sweet the chagrin we forget.


## Gleyma

Nordic 'exult', 'rejoice' that came
To mean 'forget'. Semantic leap.
A going clean out of one's head.

Blotto with joy. An ego shed
The moment my pen ghost-writes,
Such easy, couldn't-care-less

Revelling in self-forgetfulness.
Sweeney swings from birch to birch.
Birds of paradise wing within.

# Thanks

## *Thanks*

Thanks and *Danke*, *takk* and *dank*
All over the Germanic world
The same response: to think is to thank.

Indo-European *tong* 'to think
Or feel'. This root that meditates
Keeps lowering its vowel to link

Thought and gratitude, to allow
Us catch what was and is in one,
Taking a past with us into now.

## *Merci*

From Latin for 'hire' or 'fee'
Wage for services rendered
Drifts to 'favour' or 'mercy'.

No longer measure for measure
More a gift bestowed,
A giving at someone's pleasure.

One word to name and bless
A gratuitous *merci*,
Unearned openhandedness.

## 有難う
## *Arigatō*

This Japanese for 'thanks' is 'grateful';
An adjective that meant 'with difficulty'
Appreciates bother someone incurred.

Such focus on the other and the past
Apologies and gratitude have blurred
So *sumimasen* 'It isn't yet ended'

Blends 'pardon!' and 'thanks' in a word.
Sorry to have troubled you. *Arigatō.*
Deep bowings and an endless closure.


## Gracias

Spanish like Italian *grazie*
From the Latin we know in 'grace'
And 'gratitude', which in turn displays

A deeper root that meant 'to praise
Aloud' that shows again in 'bard',
'The one who lauds', 'praise-giver'.

And so I hand it to you. I deliver
My tribute, less *quid pro quo*
Than overflow. Well good for you!


## Go raibh maith agat

Longer but to the point
Irish: 'May you have good!'
Our sense of gratitude
Optatives of blessing.
Same not at all the same,

Theme with variations :
*Go dtuga Dia do shláinte dhuit!*
May God give you your health!
May God compensate you!
A calling down of gifts

谢谢
*Xièxie*

End of *gǎnxiè* 'to thank' twice
*Gǎn* for 'sense', 'feeling' or 'touch',
Its sign hearts in unison.

And *xiè* signals words and shot –
Once an arrow in a bow –
Both to show a parting shot,

A last word of emotion
Fires out a potlatch of thanks.
I'm so grateful. *Xièxie, xièxie.*


Ευχαριστίες
*Eucharisties*

Again the notion of showing favour,
*Charis* with its roots in yearning,

A thankfulness crediting generosity
As 'to bid for favour' can mean 'please'.

Daily Greek for 'please' and 'thank you'
Echo that chambered supper we renew

Shedding a cup across the centuries:
This do in remembrance of me.

Desire for what's beyond our earning
A broken bread we long to savour.

# Not At All

*Not At All!*

Oh! the airy dismissiveness in this reply –
No, not at all! Don't even mention it –
A staving off of words that seem to fly
In the face of common years of trust and sit
Uneasily with a careless take-for-grantedness
Which, although it likes to savour such
Utterances of thanks, sometimes none-the-less
Finds digesting it is almost overmuch
As if our daily assumings need a space
Where silence reigns and spares our lungs
All unneeded talk that could undo
The muted promise of any love's embrace,
Sweet nothings murmured in mother tongues:
*De nada! De res! Nakas! Pas du tout!*


とんでもない *Ton Demo Nai!*

Just *Ie! Ie!*
No! No! Or maybe to use
A *'ton demo nai'*
Meaning 'absurd', 'outrageous'
'What a thing to say!'
Good grief. Nothing of the sort.
Exaggerated
Sweeping to one side, almost
A dutiful disdain
So you start to imagine a Samurai's self-denial:
Service rendered and no nonsense.


*Gern Geschehen*

You see here how Germans don't shy away,
Or try to brush off terms of gratitude
Denying all as if to underplay
What's done, the service given poohpoohed;

But rather take this thankfulness for what
It is, a well-meant recognition of gift,
A naming of whatever someone got,
A bid to give the lifter too a lift.
My pleasure! I'd really love to do more,
Surely a favour's nothing to disown.
Then why the would-be bashful need to shun
Whatever grateful words can warm my core?
So I accept with thanks the thanks you've shown.
*Gern geschehen!* Something 'willingly done'.


## Det Skulle Bare Mangle!

Norwegian *Det skulle bare mangle!*
'It would indeed be lacking!' that's to say
What's given's simply a matter of course.

This answer to reassure both parties
To do otherwise would be to betray
A trust, to fail myself as much as you.

Remember we count on each other.
Neither of us could ever walk away
Abandoning a fallen friend to snow.


## Verði þér ad góðu!

Iceland's after meals *Verði þér að góðu!*
Like *Go ndéanaí ' mhaith duit* in Donegal
Translates simply as 'May it benefit you!' –
No dismissals here or '*Not* at all!'
Neither overmodestly self-effacing
Waving signs of gratitude aside
Or any thoughts of anxiously erasing
Each excess of thanks with Samurai pride,
More a trust in whatever has begun
Sweeping us with it and out of control
On beyond such dangers of possessing
Any feel or sense of owning favours done
As gifts and thank-yous go on changing role –
Our give and take a ricochet of blessing.

# Trusts

## Trust

Trust with roots in *deru* meaning 'steadfast',
Through India and Europe words for tree,
Latin *dūrus* for hard, heartwood to last,
Kildare 'Church of Oak' or 'grove' in Derry.
In some Germanic branches 'banking on'
Drifts to 'fellow feeling', 'a standing by' –
A shift of meaning in the lexicon:
Norwegian *trøst* both 'comfort' and 'rely',
As if our minds at rest are minds consoled
By another's word nothing undermines.
As trunk and roots steady and reassure,
The face we count on, the words that uphold
Sinkers and feeders beyond our drip lines;
No matter how long the drought oaks endure.

## Confidentia

*Confianza, confidència, confidence,*
*Con* and *fidere* 'to trust'
Latin for complete reliance,

Its root 'compel' or 'persuade'
'To be convinced', to count
On what might be betrayed.

A faith whole and entire
Bides its daring time.
You walk this taut high wire.

## Hyder

Welsh's old, now slightly literary word
With nuances: 'boldness', 'trust', 'reliance'
Which a century ago was still heard
In *ar i hyder* for 'on the off-chance'.

In origin Indo-European
For 'stretching out a hand' that comes to mean
The use of zeal or power and then to span
All the colours of meaning in between
And yet the most generous of its senses
A mark of strength, sign of extravagance
Risks how the other might misunderstand,
Take as weakness the fist that untenses,
The arm begun unfolding trust's off-chance.
Panache and daring of an outstretched hand.

## Vertrauen

German *Trost* is 'comfort'.
*Vertrauen* 'to give credence'
'To take at your word'.

*Trauen* a verb 'to trust'.
Our betrothal over
The odds. Go for bust!

Yes, my belief in you.
Ground of all love. Wager
That a word comes true.

## Lit

Mostly now in one or other compound
Scandinavian *lit* for reliance
Based on a verb 'to see' or 'look around',
Then turning noun for 'sight' or 'appearance'
That either tends to mean a 'hue' or 'sheen'
(In Icelandic 'colour' has pride of place)
Or 'sight' becomes how we ourselves are seen
By showing up at times in words for face.
Still in Norway's *Sett din lit til noen*
'Put your trust in someone' two meanings blend,
A match of face and faith that readjust
As thinking through these roots we learn again
The way we turn to countenance a friend,
Our face to face a gazing into trust.

# Friend

## *Amicus*

Latin tied to the first verb we conjugated:
*Amo, amas, amat*
I love, you love…akin to *amicus* and freighted

With our suckling recollection of *amma*
Middle Ages' Latin
'Mother', nursery petname like 'mamma'

We find again in Iceland's *amma* 'Nana'
Or Norway's wet-nurse.
Our once frost-white and honeyed manna.

*Amie, amic, amico, amigo*
Romance reflexes
Summoning every friendship in embryo,

Our naked cry of milky longing traced
From memory's womb,
Our endless desire embracing and embraced.

## *Cyfaill*

Welsh *cyfaill* 'the co-reared one' –
Our foster-sibling *comhalta* –
A companionship begun

In youth. The sweet risk and fun
Of other friends discovered
And yet all that's said and done

In our knowing inside out,
Long years of coalescence,
Breaking bread for feast or drought.

友

Japan's *tomo*,
Chinese *yău* –
As it was on the tortoise shell,
As it is now

Two hands grasped
As friendship's sign
Like a *sean-nós* singer winding
Out a line.

Hand on hand
Thick or thin.
Everything ventured, everything gained.
Win, win.


## *Vinur*

For northmen lust and trouble taken blend:
Iceland's *vinur* or Norway's *venn* for 'friend'

Stems from a root 'to strive' 'to try', 'aspire'
And so 'wish and work to achieve desire'

Both in flower-goddess Venus's sheep's-eyes.
And *fine* in Fine Gael for 'kindred allies'.

Sober northern mixture of lust and rapport,
Some irrefutable call we answer to and for.

No matter what you know I've named you friend.
The garden chosen. The seed and bloom I tend.


## *Caraid*

*Kā* as in *kamasutra* India's love tract,
An Indo-European verb 'to long'
Ah, when were such borders ever exact,
Our lines between a right and wrong?

Our western *caraid*, Welsh *cariad* for 'love'
Same root as 'charity', 'cherish' and 'whore'.
Fond caress we never get enough of
In the pith of friendship's desire for more.


## Friend

Grounded in a verb 'to hold dear or please',
Germane to 'free' and words for peace or ease

Found in Old Indian *priṇāti* 'to rejoice in',
Icelandic *frændi* once 'friend' now 'kith and kin'.

Have we not loved each other as best we could?
Of course such water became thicker than blood.

All secrets confessed under the trusted oak
Our ease and laughter a running inside joke

As rings conspire and years of roots accrue;
My friend! *Mein Freund!* I delight in you.

# GRAMMAR

Only in grammar can you be more than perfect.

WILLIAM SAFIRE

# Imperative

This inflexible linguistic strut
As speakers ask, demand, insist.
No time for doubt. A minimalist
Approach. Imperious upper hand.
No roundabout or pussyfoot.
Do exactly what I command!

Downright mood of sergeant or lover.
Nothing here but roots of verbs,
No stem or end or person curbs
Or softens. Intimate and peremptory.
Between the sheets or undercover.
Halt. About turn. Kiss me!

# Interrogative

Can you hear the courtroom voice of law?
So many ways to shape a leading question.
Weren't you there? Tell us what you saw!

You did see it, didn't you? Answer yes.
But you didn't see it, did you? Answer no.
An interrogative already a second-guess.

The barrister your father dreamt you'd be,
But cross-questions kept on fanning out
Beyond the cut and dry of dock or jury.

So much you ask yet know you can't be sure
In nuanced light and dark of inbetweenness
Your skittish themes and riffs a noodling detour.

All the *blooming buzzing confusion* you've
Called your jazz of open yes or no,
A mood to speak of things you'll never prove.

# Indicative

Simple declarative, matter of fact,
A speaker's statement 'this is how it is',
Our pointing out, unmarked modality:
A flower grows in the axil of a bract.

In any utterance no neutrality,
Everything indicative of something;
Mood for ideologue and dogmatist:
'The way I say it how it must be.'

Mood too for chroniclers and glossarists
Not in the humour for command or quiz.
Just *above my lined book birds' chanting.*
The sky is blue. I'm glad that I exist.

## Optative

*Μή γένοιτο* – May it never come about!
Greek inflections of request,
Mode of wishes.
Perish the thought!
Things sought,
Warded off or blessed,
Optings in or out.

Creaking axle shafts of prayer still turn:
May the best man win!
Long may you live!
May they rest in peace!
Desire's grease
An infinite paradigm within.
How endlessly I yearn.

# Subjunctive

A Latin term borrowed from Greek grammar
For forms of subordination we'd obey,
Those lists of conjunctions from the crammer:
French phrases with *que*, Caesar's *ut* and *ne*.
Also a stance for what's beyond our ken,
'Uncertain negatives' our rule of thumb:
*Mais hélas! je ne crois pas qu'elle vienne* –
But I'm afraid I don't believe she'll come.
Mood of but and maybe if I were you,
Tentative just supposings or surmise
And perhaps she was coming all along?
An insubordinate lover's derring-do
Chancing the riffs and pulses of surprise,
I risk what-ifs. So what if I were wrong!

# Conditional

A mood known to every Irish classroom,
*Modh coinniollach* for a hypothesis:
Either 'if I were' or 'if I had been',

A conjecture or supposition seen
From here and now how everything might be
Or might have been, opposed to how it is.

On condition something were such, then this –
A space between a future and our past,
Thought experiment, airbrushed reality.

Dream mode of reconditioned fantasy:
Were I a blackbird I'd whistle and sing,
If wishes were horses, beggars would ride.

Nightmare negatives that set now aside
Ferreting out mistakes we didn't make.
If I hadn't loved you, God alone knows.

# Progressive

*Are you agoing to Scarborough Fair?*
A view of a motion nabbed in full flight,
This song in the course of travelling where

Its love is held for years on end in play,
A balladeer pleading his jilted plight,
On York moors cries an ongoing dismay.

*Parsley, sage, rosemary and thyme*
*where water ne'er sprung nor drop of rain fell*
*And then she'll be a true love of mine...*

Sense of duration, aspect of process,
What the French describe as being in train,
Something on the go, an in-the-actness,

A verb caught up in the flow of living
Dreaming some perfection it can't attain.
Every poem a moment still on the wing.

# Habitual

In our home a forbidden paradigm.
Our parents used correct us if we said
'Does be here' to mean 'here many a time'.
*Mrs Do-be and her little does-be's*
They'd mock, insisting on saying 'is' instead,
'To be polite' just the way we'd use 'please'.

Poor Mrs Do-be didn't fill the bill.
Our habitual now a rural past,
Though some have shown it's echoed even still
In Black 'he be's here', understood as 'daily'
Or 'often' – habit and now in contrast,
Hidden dissonance in jazz or *céilí*.

We learned our Irish endings off by rote:
*Éirím, cuirim orm mo chuid éadaí...*
I rise, I dress, I eat, I sit and I devote
Whatever allotment of years head bent
Over this page. O does-be monkish me
In love with my habitual present.

# Perfective

All those parallel pairs of Slavic verbs:
'I read it' or 'I read it to the end',
One the act, the other its completion.

Less the time than the contours of doing,
A gazing at aspects of the deed itself,
A perfectionist conjuring fulfilment.

So much begun that's still not quite finished,
Learning this and that, never 'having learned',
Same old yearning to say a work is done.

Once more this cluttered table cleared
Believing again hope's guardian angel
And this time I know I will have read...

Flawed stop-start flow. Faultless tomorrow.
Imperfect pasts, dreams of perfect futures.

## Recent Perfect

I've just eaten a mango zipped with lime,
So recent and perfect my lips still twang.
*Gerade*, just now, finished or come from –
*Ah! Je viens de manger une grosse mangue* –
Only or barely, no mention of time.

On Celtic fringes a like idiom
Conscious of time 'we're after eating'
Reflects an Irish *th'éis* or Welsh *wedi*,
Prepositions that qualify fleeting
Verbal nouns with their temporal aplomb

And hold in suspense the passing heady
Moment to invoke stings of pleasure fresh
In the mouth while still the corrosive lime
Bites slivers of a phantom mango's flesh.
Around my tongue juices whirl and eddy.

# Frequentative

Angles of vision that enhance
Heightened eyescape of lovers,
Seeing the parts and whole at once.

Aspect we didn't learn at school,
How *–er* turns a flick to flicker,
How a constant drip is dribble.

O that sudden flare of fancy,
And how at the start you'd startled
Falling for the same frequency.

Weight of any vowel we utter,
Intensity of syllables,
One more sound and chat is chatter.

To dab and dabble and so mate.
Frequentative of *habere* 'have'
In where we dwell, our habitat.

Sparkle of what first sparked us off.
Moist firewood cracked, then crackled
Kindling such inhabitable love.

# Future

Futures go back to a fifth form at school.
*Amabo*, *Amabis*, 'I'll love', 'you'll love',
Bulldog conducting the air with his rule,
Favourite Latin tense to rattle off.

Then, our Irish future written with *f*s
*Molfaidh mé*, *molfaidh tú*, 'I'll praise', 'you'll praise',
These eulogies amid exams and biffs,
Anapaests and dactyls the pulse obeys.

Strange to speak of an English 'future tense',
A term Germanic languages borrow;
Like Japanese, adverbs carry the sense:
We meet today and we part tomorrow.

For most only a present and a past –
Both 'we will' or 'we shall' our current moods –
The things we wish or want or may forecast,
A modal giving up on certitudes.

Here's the tense where a time and fancy cross
In loving and praising beyond our ken;
We wager on tomorrow's pitch and toss,
Our future still a mood of mice and men.

# Past

The past a car's rear-mirror glanced,
A glimpsed once-off, an aorist dream,
The roadway's cloud of dust behind,
The arrow of now already advanced,
A point in time's reflected gleam
Almost out of my sight and mind.

What is, what was and what's to come
Just one more way of seeing things –
The Hopi split their moods in three:
Timeless truth (like four's the sum
Of three and one), so happenings
(I read), what's still uncertainty.

The pedal down I'm speeding on.
A tense or mood it's all so fast,
So much to say that's still unsaid.
A flickered mirror image gone
As yet another bend slides past
And swallows up the road ahead.

# Pluperfect

Here in the Natural History Museum
From Loch Gur, Naglack. Ballebetagh knuckle-necked
Giant Irish deer, a portal-keeping threesome,
Show off their skeleton key to our past perfect.
With Ireland, Britain and mainland Europe still linked
They'd arrived from Asia twelve thousand years ago;
Largest antlers of all deer living or extinct,
Frozen out they'd died like a second-floor dodo.
So strange how a *had* rounds off all halcyon days
Of a perfect past where such specimens had been
One casualty of nature's planned obsolescence;
A *floruit* complete before a climate phase
In their ebony cage of air a long lost gene
Forever exuding its own pluperfect tense.

# Causative

The weight of just one syllable,
How even the shapes of a tongue
Make of an intransitive verb
The cause and because of action,

Though often a roundabout way
With another phrase: I'll have you
Know the rain will make the tree grow,
*La pluie fait pousser l'arbre,*

Some like Japanese or Finnish
Juggle letters, add a suffix,
A self-contained moving spirit
Inflected in the word itself.

But now fossilised in English
Like trees we fell before they fall
Their trunks laid where they lie frozen,
A layer of verbs as 'sit' and 'set',

Where lowered vowels give rise to change,
Raise a forebear's remembered sap
To work such subtle shift in sound,
Ghost in us their shadow patterns.

# Potential

Each time I hear a Japanese potential
It brings to mind that nun I never met
Who'd ask her friends to name five unlived dreams,
Then ticking off the list she'd ask why not?

*Naru* 'become', *nareru* 'can become,
Can grow, emerge, turn out or come to be' –
But 'can' is much too moody and detached,
An auxiliary so like 'may' or 'might'.

Too many pallid years of asking why.
All our endless brief postponements have left
At first a rift and then a cosy gap
Between our modals and infinitive

So we define ourselves too narrowly,
Saying how we'd love to but never could,
As if we want to make our lack our dream,
Until it seems we'd rather fade than flourish.

But no excuses! Why not? An ending
That binds its potential into the verb.
*Saku* 'to bloom' and *sakeru* 'can bloom,
Open or blossom or come into flower'.

# Active Voice

The mode for inflecting a verb
With subject as action-taker,
The doer of whatever's done.

Endings to indicate the one
Concerned is mover and shaker,
Protagonist of the scene.

For years before St Stephen's Green
Despair forestalled dark with dark,
Gloomy failure in self-defence,

A subject's still verbless sentence.
O resurrection in a park,
Spring and sunlight your leitmotif,

Madness in each unfolded leaf.
Unclenching, another young spark
Dares the inflections of a voice.

# Middle Voice

Classic Greek or Icelandic halfway voice,
Subject as gainer, both setter and scene:
*Ég gleðst* 'I delight myself', 'rejoice',
Not active, not passive, but in between.
*Feromai* 'I carry off', on the make
The doers and their benefit cohere,
Sometimes reflexive, others give and take,
*þeir heilsast hér*, they greet each other here.
Self-possessed verbs for a pivotal time,
Neither old nor young, belonging to each,
The days when still we tuned into both spheres
As two generations bridged in our prime
Were greeting one another within reach.
My middle voice delighted in those years.

## Passive Voice

Subjects once the actors and achievers
Learn the lonely voice of ghosts that hover,
The fathers of our youth who slip beyond.

Here we're turned by 'by' into receivers,
In handing and being handed over
The active voice and passive correspond.

Beckoned again, taken and still amazed
Such a range of verbs allow surrender,
Leaving us less the mover than the moved.

Years of action, even attainments praised,
So no need for feats or proofs of gender
Just let one lover enjoy being loved.

Our balance tips and wants to smile and bow
In going with what we must undergo,
Live and let live of things best left unsaid.

Our fathers gone. Are we the fathers now?
Like Rilke's angels we often do not know
If we walk among the living or the dead.

# Conjugation

After our meat and wine
Again the time, the voice and mood combine
For conjugation,
Come-hither invitation,
I can't decline.

Latin lover's tense,
*Amo, amas, amat* – consummate nonsense,
Charms of grammar,
Source of all glamour,
Rhythm's accidence.

A verb to x-rate –
Steady now Bulldog don't exaggerate –
As we chant
*Amamus, amatis, amant.*
Let's conjugate.

Imperative but tender
*Ama!* Single command of either gender.
Love me.
Subject, inflect, perfect me
In my surrender.

# Concessive

These clauses begin granting that although
They take subjunctives in many grammars –
*Bien que je ne puisse pas réussir,*

Even if (it may be) I can't succeed –
They hold concessions somehow in the air,
Let's suppose world of might or might not be

In spite of which still something else is true.
Although we know we've always fallen short
And while this may be the gist of yearning,

As if by laws of increasing returns
Desire expands to meet increased desire,
We keep on conjuring up fulfilments.

*Then who under heaven have I but you?*
For all my vanities and brokenness,
It's you I've loved all my livelong days.

# Infinitive

To wake, to love, to dance, to be, to do –
Unmarked tense or person, unencumbered
English underdetermined point of view,
Non-committal dictionary headword.
Both substantive and verb, a borderland,
For Irish or Turkish only a noun,
In Tokyo the subject hearers understand,
While Portuguese lets pronouns tie it down.
Undefined shifting inbetweenness,
A spirit here and now that yet can soar,
Verbal action and a noun's sereneness,
Movement and stillness at the dance's core.
Beside incarnate person, number, mood,
A silence in the verb to be, infinitude.

# Comparative

Were geraniums redder than the rose?
A childhood nagging to like one better.
Odd how I can't remember which I chose,

The roses' flame, the geraniums' flare?
Bit redder, redder, reddest, real reddest,
Lithuanian's five grades to compare.

Upping the pace we're gathering unease,
Fast, faster, big, bigger and biggest,
Worlds haunted by comparative degrees.

Japanese superlatives use *ichiban* –
The number one this, the number one that –
In all comparisons a silent 'than'.

Than you. Than me. Such an urge to compete,
Yet still somehow adequate, unique, whole.
Can anything be more or less complete?

This is my moment, my place in the sun.
Shine the geranium, shine the wild rose.
All incomparable under the One.

# Reflexive

'I see myself' – a folding back to where
Subject and object allude to one thing,

'Doer', the patient to whom verbs refer,
Body implied when I say I'm shaving.

This pronoun 'self' reflects long tangled roots:
The *swa* in *swaraj*, the *Féin* in *Sinn Féin*,

'Sib' in sibling, the 'eth' in ethnic roots,
one's own man in King Henry's 'homely swain'.

Reflex that's my own I learned to acquire
In years of overwhelmings I'd withstood,

In ravelled nodes of memory and desire,
Alongside the other, my frail selfhood.

One apprenticeship in our lovely mess
*Sui generis* of lifelong labour,

Reeled in psychic thread of shifting sameness,
Self I love so I can love my neighbour.

# Suppletive

Unknowingly we grow into grammar,
Absorbing freaks in our newfound patterns,
*My Daddy goed to his work this morning*
As littler, littlest yield to less and least
And learn how fathers went or wended there.

Other words as stopgaps in inflections –
*Bon, meilleur, le meilleur*, good, better, best;
*Tháinig* 'came', *tagann* 'comes', *tiocfaidh* 'will come';
Latin's *fero, ferre, tuli, latum,*
*Fero* 'I bear' mixed with *tollo* 'I lift'.

Evenings we passed swotting principal parts.
Nothing exotic in the abnormal
Come-day, go-day of the commonest things,
The irregular born by frequency,
Strangeness hidden in the ordinary

As it was in the beginning, is now
And ever shall be. Eternal echo.
*Is, was* that meant 'to stay, dwell, pass a night'
And *be* 'to exist, to grow, to become'
One suppletive. Three verbs interwoven.

# Possessive

Word now smeared with green-eyed innuendo –
Desires to keep another under thumb –
Here an older genitive's afterglow
In possessive *s*'s *ad libitum*.
A friend's friend's face I imagine I know,
Germanic *s* links our genitive chain,
Nouns gather up each other as they go,
A network of relations set in train.
But traces of possession elsewhere too:
*His* and *hers* genitives of *he* and *she* –
These personal pronouns we still decline –
*Ours* possessive of *we* and *yours* of *you*
Marking what we love grammatically.
*I know that I am yours and you are mine.*

# Consecutive

First a main clause with *such*, *enough* or *so*
Stating what's true to this or that degree,
A comma, then the consequences flow.

One thing is such, the other follows suit:
Our lives so brief that every moment sings;
Consecutives one statement bearing fruit.

Classic Greek marks off – and German likewise –
Fact from guess, reserving infinitives
Or subjunctive modes to signal surmise.

For most a mood indicative of fact,
Choice by choice we flap our butterfly wings;
Things were such, this is how we had to act.

So far, so good. Judgements made in pauses,
Each choice a breath in our delivery,
Our lives lived in consecutive clauses.

*Yet knowing how may leads on to way*:
The pulse of words, my birds of paradise
I loved so much, I'm still this child at play.

# Relative

*A lamp is placed midways on a spaceship*
*Which moves at a speed relative to Mars,*
*As the midpoint passes Observer One,*
*Who stands on the planet, a light flashes*
*Which another watcher who stands on board –*

Lamps, spaceship, observer, light and watcher
All topics to headline our attention
Until they yield to 'which' or 'who' or 'that'
Until their tale unfolds in relatives
Where they move and flash and have their being.

But there are worlds with no relative clause,
Instead, for instance, a longer adjective,
So 'a watcher who stands on board' becomes
'An-on-board-standing watcher' in Japan.
How our relatives are relativised!

*– Observer Two, sees at the stern and bow*
*At once, while for One they are out of sync,*
*Stern before bow because the ship has moved.*
All motion relative to the seer,
The constant that I trust, the speed of light.

# Gender

Has gender now taken a carnal turn,
More to do with sex than *der*, *die* and *das*
Or the list of endings we had to learn,
*Die See, der See* mugged up before a class?
For most grammars it meant different things:
Animate or not, the shape of objects;
Indo-European in its beginnings
Must have slowly aligned its nouns with sex.
Those paradigms and gender never squared –
Neuter *Mädchen* a strange anomaly –
Far more than what divides us we'll have shared,
As I'm manning you, you're womaning me.
An inner likeness grows ripe and tender,
Our years flexing towards a common gender.

## Subordination

Although for any kite there's wind enough,
Since I can feel a breeze against my cheeks,
As if you'd wafted a Japanese fan,
In order to recall that summer park,
Where father showed me how to fly a kite...

Dreams' unanchored subordinate clauses
Drift through the undergrowth of a psyche;
A complex sentence held in suspension
Like a lengthy learned German sentence,
Patiently waits to find its main clause.

Subordination? A strange word for us
That echoes from father's generation
Parsed and analysed prepositions
Which still govern the accusative case,
The supine or checking the agreement.

*My father in the night commanding no.*
And so the fancy-led years of freedom,
Moving with one current then the other;
Although for any kite there's wind enough,
Any stringless winged box scuds and plunges.

How many years to learn a discipline
To set 'althoughs' and 'as ifs' in order?
Like a main clause, desire subordinates
Each gentle pulling back to soar again.
My hand holds a kite tense against the wind.

# First Person

## *Singular*

The node of all our Western nodes,
Me, me and me of big egos,
Subject of most episodes.

In Japanese 'I' rarely shows –
No need to mention you or me –
From the context everyone knows.

In doubt, a pause for modesty,
Forefinger raised to tip the nose:
*Watashi desu ka?* Is it me?

## *Plural*

'We' as nominative and 'us' the oblique.
As with 'I' and 'me' no known connection,
A Proto-Indo-European freak.

Insider *wareware*, we the group,
We the company, we the Japanese,
We, we only, dangerously cock-a-hoop.

Of course, Royal We. But some like Malay
Or Oceanic tongues contrast between
'We' as 'you-and-me' and 'I-and-they'.

Gauguin's cherried women in Tahiti
I imagine turning to a lover
Murmuring this sweetest pronoun 'you-and-me'.

# Second Person

## *Singular*

Whatever happened to *thee*, *thy* and *thou*
*Who art in heaven, hallowed be thy name*

*Thy kingdom come, thy will be done on earth?*
So intimately we speak to our God,

Like Walter Morel's Nottingham lingo
*Look thee at it, tha niver wants ter shake.*

'You' or 'yer' to priest, 'thou' or 'tha' for friends,
A plural for respect like *vous* or *Sie*,

Until in the end all are speaking proper
With only prayers or traces in England's north.

## *Plural*

Once accusative and dative of 'ye',
'You', old plural of 'thou', a standard use
Blotting out all else, or so it may seem,

But bubbling underground another dream.
The school uproars of 1968
Brought back Europe's youth our *tu* and *Du*.

'Thou' and 'thee' a loss too late to undo,
Instead new plurals in the undergrowth:
America's 'y(ou) all', 'y(ou) ones', 'you guys'.

Given Irish *tú* and *sibh* no surprise
Common Ireland's plurals 'ye', 'yous' and 'yiz'
With 'yous' now striking roots in Liverpool.

A grammar shifts along its sliding rule
As fresh plurals grant a singular 'you'.
A craved intimacy, our need for *thou*.

# Third Person

In every utterance a 'you' and 'me',
The third person somehow an afterthought,
Outside our orbit 'they' or 'she' and 'he'

Interlopers in any triangle.
Indo-European fails to tally
*Er und Sie, han og hun* or *il et elle*,

Cobbled from words for 'that' or 'this' or 'yon',
'This lassie' and 'that one' and 'yon fellow',
Now rooted deeply in our lexicon.

In Japanese for years 'that person there'
Until to translate Europe's novels' 'he',
*Kare* 'that one' and almost unaware

A language gains *kare* and *kanojo*
For 'he' and 'she' though they still summon up
Other undertones of 'girlfriend' or 'beau'.

Possessive timbres in this 'he' or 'she'
Desire to delight in just their saying.
A lover's name drops between you and me.

# Relative Antecedent

A mouthful generations learned in class:
Nouns 'who', 'whose', 'which' or 'that' stand for,
Words so close they're each other's alias,
Two subjects of clauses in full rapport.
Bond both relative and unrelated,
Two parts that both blend and keep a selfhood –
Kinship both embedded and complicated –
Where water's every drop as thick as blood.
One who unknowingly I'd journeyed to,
One for whom it seems my being was meant,
One whose time and mine together unfold,
One that I speak of now, of course, is you,
My only relative antecedent,
One whom I promise still to love and hold.

# UNDER THE SIGN

*Le symbole donne à penser.*

The symbol gives rise to thought.

PAUL RICŒUR, *La Symbolique du mal*

# Heart

A reduced four-stroke pictogram,
Just some vague suggestions,
The subtlest hints or faint outlines,
Traces of ventricles;
A health logo or Valentine,
Metaphor for every
Shaded nuance of heart and mind,
'Spirit', 'thought', 'will' or 'care'.

Pacemaker. Pump-room.
Sign for what we bear in mind,
Things we take to heart.

No longer used alone to mean
The cardiac organ;
Umbrella word for heart and mind
That we've divided up:
Brain box and sensibility,
Affections and psyche,
A hard-wiring and a software
All under the one sign.

A heart reminded
Heartening its lonely mind.
A mended oneness.

# Worry

### 1

First left a minimalist stylisation
Of a heart, first organ in our embryo
Blood-pump and relay station.

And next to the left a jar of vino
At the right a figure on his knees
Maybe pouring it out to show

Dispersal. Together 'anxieties',
*Shinpai* 'worry', to undergo
A divided heart, a mind's unease.

### 2

Bird of my spirit gone into spin,
Round and round a rim of sanity.
Unnumbered hair. Fallen sparrow.

'Angst' and 'anguish' words for narrow.
The diffuse closes off in anxiety,
A widening out, a shrinking in.

So much caring too diluted, too thin.
This wine jar forever half-empty.
Scattered heart. Sapped marrow.

### 3

A figure bent and busy at the jar
Pumping adrenalin in a worry gland.
An endless night, closed and circular.

O sandman break the ring of doubt
As surrendering again to the unplanned
A concentration broadens out.

Whole-hearted. All-embracing.
Blake's single grain of sand.
Carefree loving of one thing.

意　I

# Thought

### 1

The upper portion makes up a sign for sound:
What was a needle shows a passing through
Over a mouth and tongue. The strokes hung

Below, a heart. Thoughts and likings wrung
Out of the core's pump and pulse to imbue
The lonely mind. Our caring's middle ground:

Neither *Rausch* nor Nietzsche's will unbound.
Heart and mind. Needle-sharp. Steel-true.
A heart full of sounds with a ready tongue.

### 2

Light of reason against the shades of doubt,
A steely dream of certainty we wanted to find.
The pulse was a flirt, the heart a gadabout,

Think and therefore be like René Descartes!
Four strokes out of sight and out of mind,
At bottom a forlorn sound was losing heart.

Top and underside stepping out of line,
Hinted wisdom of a symbol undermined,
Our centuries pass under a fractured sign.

### 3

Every either-or more our loss than gain.
Stumbling *homo sapiens* divider and tilter
At windmills, trying to draw a perfect line

Between things that willy-nilly still combine.
World of twoness too long out of kilter.
From the heart's safe-deposit a richer vein,

A murmur mouthed in a needle eye of brain,
Currency of give and take; our flow and filter
Safe and sound under one mended sign.

味 AJI

# Taste

### 1

Side by side and here working as a pair:
A mouth and a tree topped with newly sprung
Branches for what's unfinished or left in the air.

*Aji* (or in compounds *mi*), a shoot twanging
Our taste-buds, tang of grape that has clung
To the palate, twinge of pleasure left hanging.

Slack and slop of liquid easing a drouth
A gulp remembering its turn around a tongue,
Something good lingering here in the mouth.

### 2

Even taste has its roots in a verb 'to touch',
The wine-kissed lips, the tongue caressed,
Of all our five senses this is the apogee.

A foretaste already enjoyed in what we see
Before we relish an aroma along with the zest,
Delighting in the bouquet just as much.

Our savouring hardly just one sense as such
But combining four the most rooted and loftiest,
These taste-buds surely at the top of the tree.

### 3

Our foretaste a tree still about to sprout,
Our aftertaste as much memory as learning,
The sense both recollects and branches out.

A meaning ramifies, growing now to imply
A certain feel for excellence, skill in discerning,
A nose for what's worthwhile, a weather eye.

In gastric juices, in a bud's tangy secretion
A taste for the unfinished business of yearning,
Our growing sense of growing incompletion.

意味  IMI

# Meaning

### 1

So the signs for thought and taste together:
An idea chewed on long enough to find
The pith and gist that seem to linger whether

By choice or dint of whatever tang of hope
Or memory coalesce and shape inside the mind,
A kind of double-think that needs to grope

Behind and beyond a naked present tense
For meaning, first zest and savour combined,
Our double character trying to make sense.

### 2

Futures grasped too quickly, moves too rash,
All our histories of lust for a simpler sign.
It's brain and body and no overweening

Mind, rather a sense of lives spent gleaning
Mood to mood clues and tokens of design
Caught between the back and forward flash

In day by day of love's unwatched panache,
A career of frames become one storyline,
In flickers of our moments, hints of meaning.

### 3

Among the five why choose the sense of taste?
Why not the sign for sight or hearing instead
Or even our limbs recall of loves embraced?

What of Proust's taunting scents that clung
To every bygone Eden? Too much head –
Let the flesh and juices kiss the tongue

Till appetite is both foretaste and residue;
In this sense desire becomes a memory fed,
Feedback of meaning in all we mean to do.

# Master

### 1

This emblem's origin still easily recognised:
In the single slanted stroke above you see
The blaze of a wick wavering just a bit

Above an oil lamp carefully stemmed to sit
Plump upwards, gleaming its own authority,
A simple pictograph only a little stylised,

A Freudian symbol hardly even disguised.
Only the flame shivers in the draft of history
As on a master's orders the lamps are lit.

### 2

The owner alone decided when at nightfall
To order oil lamps trimmed and lit to shine
Glories of his house and home. A boss's call.

Eyebrows raised to an underling, as if to say
'I hold sway here and all you see is mine',
A gesture of power, an understated display.

And there it stands upright, downright oil lamp,
The leftward skew of its flame a nodding sign
Of power, its master's sanction, seal and stamp.

### 3

Lord or owner, employer and a whole train
Of meanings: spirit, husband, darling, you,
Prime, head, foremost, chief and main.

Now less a lantern and more like a candlestick
But for five millennia a symbol of overview;
Five brush strokes and one imagined wick

An icon of mastery for a fourth of humankind
Drifts and gains a nuance or shifts its hue;
An image glows in the lamp-rooms of mind.

注意　CHŪI

# Attention

### 1

Three water-drops and the oil lamp that there
Stands for 'column' or 'upright', a long spout
That seems almost to form a shaft in mid-air

As it falls, to show a liquid's downward flow
And give the sense of something pouring out.
Then there's the ideogram for 'thought' to show.

A lavished mind! Two signs mark the need
Of a single-mindedness. No wobble or doubt.
This steady pouring over and taking heed.

### 2

How so rich a meaning begins to overflow!
'Attention' but as much 'to observe', 'to note' –
Our cooler need to record whatever we know.

Lovely leakage and seeping of each meaning
As nuance after nuance starts to drift and float:
'To care', 'to take an interest' and as if leaning

Over to tend we're watching and watch out for,
So 'to guard' or 'warn' that then may connote
'To caution' or 'advise'. A spillage of rapport.

### 3

Every shift of meaning yet a tighter bond,
A courtship in some kind of sliding metaphor
Of thoughtfulness splashing from a sign above

And pouring over what we're thinking of.
A logic of attention allows no either/or,
A sense of concentration streaming beyond

Itself as meanings tumble out to correspond.
How this taking care becomes our caring for;
Our daily tendings now tending towards love.

119

## To Show

### 1

Once a pictograph of a roughly made
Altar with drops of blood on either side
(or splashes of sacred wine?), above laid

Out flat over the top some sacrifice.
And so a verb-ending. Some dove-eyed
Victim on a table or any object of price?

Signs of overflow. A shedding or spill.
Tributes paid trying to bridge the divide
As humans ask the gods to show their will.

### 2

A hieroglyphic so pared back and stern,
Hiding behind an image hidden away,
Stroke by stroke reveals for us its meaning.

Hints and omens of our gods intervening
To show their will. Drawings by their protégés
Down by the Yellow Riverside still yearn

For a sign on which all other showings turn.
Any action hangs on this divine display,
A holy show making sense of everything.

### 3

Dreams of five millennia curve and flow
To bend over an altar's unspoken word
Begging moment by moment gods to show

A sign of revelation, any token to appease
Our inborn yearning. O tired heart stirred
By a curtain's twitch or a voice in a warm breeze!

The hints we find or choose to make our own,
Sounds once listened for become what's heard;
The omen sought, the only omen shown.

啓示 KEIJI

# Revelation

### 1

A door on its post, a hand on a cane
(Implying force) and beneath these
An opening as if to underscore

How someone was prepared to ignore
A rebuff and intrude. Then comes a Chinese
Reading for 'show' as *ji*. In vain

The visitor who knocked tries to gain
Entrance. Anything just to squeeze
Past the jamb. A foot in heaven's door.

### 2

Won't-take-no-for-an-answer guest,
This door-stepper skulking outside
Refuses to settle for second best,

Persists in medleys of praise and grouse
Whose trust in the host is always implied;
Awkward customer, bother-the-house

Who love-bombs or pesters if needs be,
With grit and neck of a psalmist who cried
*How long wilt thou hide thy face from me?*

### 3

To haunt a door-sill in heaven's name
As the loyal suitor always on call,
A votary waiting to stake a claim.

No quick come-on or *quid pro quo*.
No cupboard love. The long haul
Of a courtship's slow touch and go

As though even the host is lonely
Those moments before revealing all.
This need to be loved for love only.

# Sage

### 1

The upper part a conventionalised ear
On the left side, an orifice on the right
(Formerly an open mouth) and here

To denote an attentive ear-hole. Below
A man is standing on the earth, upright
And alert (suggesting clarity) and so

This combination shows us a tableau
Of vigilance, an image used to write
'Sage', 'wise ruler', 'saint' or 'maestro'.

### 2

Chinese reading *sei* also means 'holy',
A trait seen in such figures long ago
Intent on hearkening to the still unsaid.

Their range of the attentive single-minded:
Sage, wise ruler, saint and maestro
With years of obedience, decades slowly

Tuning in, whole lifetimes spent solely
To pluck from the air a half-heard tremolo,
Upright and up to their ears in the sacred.

### 3

But what on earth can it be that's clear?
A hint, a whisper, a murmuring which
Will never allow them turn a deaf ear,

A sound more a shiver than any sound,
A tuning fork's discerning twitch,
Upright though with an ear to the ground?

Yet something is clearly to be heard.
The wise man stands there at fever pitch,
Still all ears for some unearthly word.

指導　SHIDŌ

# Leading

### 1 HAND

From the Yellow River to Japan a learning how
Generations of brushstrokes could
Signal 'leadership' in two characters allied.

*Shi* 'a finger' or 'pointing': a hand alongside
A sign for 'tasty' or simply 'good'
Whose sound may well suggest 'branch' or 'bough'

With *dō*: above a symbol for 'the way' or *tao*,
Below 'a measure' and understood
As a sage or skilful hand to lead or guide.

### 2 HANDS-ON

Headway of a vessel in rhythm;
*Let the sea roar and all that fills it,*
Still to tune and trim

And believe a crew's feedback
That feeds forward, a kinship of feeling
When to harden or slack,

Trusting nothing can overwhelm,
Wonder of moving in phase and yet
A lone hand at the helm.

### 3 HANDOVER

To give it all and still the wisdom to know
How things nurtured steer from inside.
To praise and let go,

A stage well run, to call it then a day
And time a perfect handing over.
At the crux of a relay

One peaks as another hits his stride.
A baton slid from hand to hand.
Glory of standing aside.

經驗 KEIKEN

# Experience

### 1

Beside a generic symbol for any thread
(Tangled skeins) and three warps on a loom
To get the idea of something passing through.

On the right another character with two
Parts: a steed sideways-on with a plume
For a tail, a lid (consensus) on a double-head

Of two people talking. A horse inspected
To express 'examine'. Signs for *keiken* assume
We're observing as we go everything we do.

### 2

*Kei* a warp or also a line of longitude.
What is, what was, what's yet to come,
The traverse knit of our precious latitude.

Aware or half-aware our interwoven being
Patterns and hues of whatever we become.
A longwise tying down, a sideways freeing.

Lengths of thread spool out our existence.
Over and under of crossed thread and thrum
A daily texture, our weftage of experience.

### 3

Never seeing both sides of patterns we weave,
Our crossovers a passing through, going under
What's undergone and still not losing the thread.

Lookers in the gift horse's mouth have doubted.
Moment by moment the eternities we plunder,
Given moments rifled and watched as we leave.

Both a letting-go and being on the *qui vive*
As riding a moment's spur we heed the wonder;
An unplanned happening so carefully inspected.

期 KI

# Period

A winnower beside a moon
(Once a sun underneath),
A device to sift chaff by wind
As symbol of harvests
And a pitted oblong crescent.
'Period', 'time', 'date', 'term'
Measured in months and winnowings
To tab season and year.

Reapers marking time.
Husks wafting from the grain
Under August moons.

World of lunar rings and phases –
Not yet the glacial tick
Or the noiseless digital watch
Twitching arrows of time –
Still a dream moving in its seed,
Grain growing out of dark
As generations take their turn,
A blind date with the light.

Chaff riding the wind.
Rhythmic winnowing of time.
Our term's wax and wane.

情　JŌ

# Feeling

A form of heart beside what was
A plant over a well
Now modified implies 'blue-green'
Or simply 'fresh' and 'young'.
This combination comes to mean
'Feeling', or just 'passion'.
Renewed springs and stirrings of sap.
A moist and pliant core.

Straight and true-hearted.
Blue-green of plants near water.
A shoot unfolding.

This word for feeling branches out
In lush outgrowths of sense:
'Warmheartedness' or 'affection',
'Sentiment', 'emotion'
And even comes to mean a 'fact',
A 'truth'. Clear-eyed. Hard-nosed.
Things touched. Things palpable and true.
What's tangible and real.

Both feeling and fact.
Fresh and green and tenable.
A heart's roots watered.

# Word

### 1

Over what was once like a grin,
Now this squared-off mouth, four
Strokes piled up on top, a vapour

Of sounds that widen then taper
Off in a shortened stave before
Vanishing; earlier a sign for 'pin'

Or 'needle' to mean a honing in,
A tongue's tip both flap and door,
A breath-stopper and noise-shaper.

### 2

Mind and tongue's twin thrill
As taste-buds wrap around
A vowel, muscling in until

Meaning and voice coincide,
Caressing the right word found.
Inner hum heard on the outside

As messenger and message unite.
Lips pursed for a kiss of sound.
Mouth pleasured. Utter delight.

### 3

For Greeks a living principle, a force,
A reading of our universe as much
As something said or a message sent.

Here nothing so ample was meant
Or any broader sense as such,
More an articulation than a source,

A noise decoded in due course,
A mouth-music played by touch,
Stave of sound-waves in their ascent.

## Human

Side-view of *homo sapiens*
Once bending with arms down
Now matchstick torso striking out,
Stark and upright earthling,
A figure striding, God knows where.
Springy twiglike upside-down Y.
A wishbone. A divining rod.
*Hito*. Human. *Ein Mensch.*

Naked and maskless.
Here neither female nor male.
A bare-boned biped.

And yet a self-reflecting mind.
At first two downward strokes
Inscribed on bone or tortoise shell,
A bare pictograph.
Bit by bit crisscross of symbols
Living lives of their own,
A pointing out and interplay,
A signal's doubleness.

Grounded sign-maker,
High-minded and down-to-earth.
Our human being.

信  SHIN

# Trust


A human body sideways on
With arms and legs aligned;
Two-stroke Picasso matador,
One upright, one tilted,
Beside the character for speech,
A plain symbol for 'trust',
'truth', 'confidence', 'sincerity',
'reliance', 'devotion'.

*Homo erectus*,
A promiser and truster
Standing by a word.

And for all the Trojan horses,
Pledges kept or broken,
A stranger standing at the gate,
Our fragile city's guest
Barefaced and alone with a sign.
Trust's all or nothingness.
One forlorn figure and a word.
Spoken collateral.

So here then I stand
At least as good as my word.
You can count on me.

優しい   YASASHII

# Gentle

### 1

A man walking and a head over a heart
Over an upturned foot that once meant
A dancer performing a slow ritual dance

Until skilfulness tipped a meaning's balance
To 'actor' or 'excellence' which in turn lent
The nuance 'gentle' – mastery's counterpart.

*Yasashii*: 'kindly', 'with a tender heart',
Its suffixed pot-hanger and ditto of hooks bent
Inward to spell this adjective's loving stance.

### 2

A friend at four score and ten –
Twenty over the Book's allotment –
Celebrates autumn over again.

Delighted with everything but of late
Paring back to the naked present
Where the head and heart and gait

Of such mastery now move with less
Motion, this gentle dancer intent
On zeroing in on a dance's stillness.

### 3

A richer twinkling each time we meet,
A dance of stars beyond our ken,
Still with us but glinting stillness.

Deep, deeper, deepest. Endless
Comparative degrees down in a Zen
Of self. *Yasashii* as you greet

Another birthday's bittersweet
When the sumac and maples redden
Gently as a word so full of *s*'s.

火　HI

# Fire

So much more a spark than a blaze,
A glitter of friction.
Earlier a triple peaked crown
From a story-book king,
A sign on an oven button;
Three jagged tongues of flame
Usurping the blank air.

Suddenly a blitz
As out of rubbed nothingness
Steel and flint spit fire.

Tinder-box of paradox.
Coldest flint, hottest fire,
Riskiest of all elements,
A danger to play with.
Enough to warm not to consume;
A kept fire burns the most.
Still the impromptu blare of tongues,
Quick thrill of a flare-up.

The feared damp fire-stick.
Such flint-eyed moments scraped for.
A bidden spark flies.

談　DAN

## Talk

Word and then those two signs for fire
On top of each other
For the most part to indicate
-*itis* 'inflammation',
But here to catch the flash-over,
A wordage set alight,
Instantaneous combustion,
Our talking like blazes.

Flamboyance of speech.
A spirited discussion.
Our words flaring up.

*Dan* – more often used in compounds:
*Sōdan* 'mutual talk',
'Consultation', tinder of words,
Sudden kindling of thought,
Poised somewhere in a back-and-forth
Of our inbetweenness.
A speaker and a receiver,
This two-way ignition.

Dialogue. Brainstorm.
Our sparking off each other.
Word-*itis*. Tongues of fire.

霊 REI

# Spirit

Raindrops spilling out of the skies,
Below a shamanness
Working into her ecstasy
So the spirit descends:
A 'soul', a 'ghost' or 'memory',
Whatever's wafting above,
A drive, quiver of energy,
A departed essence.

The heavens opened;
An abandon summoning
Downpours of spirit.

Through a rapture or reverie
In soughs of memory
The shade of a forebear conjured
Out of heaven knows where,
A character showing spirit,
Engine, *élan vital*,
Kick-start, quickness, urge to exist,
The bird flying within.

Earthling, skyscraper
In this magical oneness.
Panache of being.

言霊  KOTODAMA

## Spirit of a Language

Word-spirit, soul of a language,
Speech-psyche, goblin tongue,
Genius of a past still within,
Old marvels shaping us
In echo-chambers of our ghosts,
Distant ventriloquists
Throwing across our centuries
Timbres of their own voice.

Ease and surety
Of our given living-room.
Take-for-granted tongue.

All that's familiar and certain
But changing as we speak
Accumulating slippages,
Our half-unconscious shifts,
Patterns slowly rearranging
We mimic and absorb
Passing on such small accruals,
Our mark left unbeknownst.

Elfish go-between.
Spirit-rapping medium.
Brokered gift of tongues.

# World

### 1

A cross means ten and here three
Share a transverse; at the foot of two
A right-angled bar just added on.

Those thirty years before a baton
Passes and creation begins anew:
'Age', 'era', 'world', 'society'.

A downward branch on a family tree.
A lap run. A closure and a début.
Another generation already gone.

### 2

Ten to soak in life unknowingly,
Ten to unravel all unknowing,
Ten in years you're still fancy-free

To own the globe. Out of the blue
A generation has come tiptoeing,
Stealing gently up behind you.

The way of the world. *Yo no narai.*
A coming that grows into a going.
Then three decades by and by.

### 3

And suddenly it's your sixtieth year.
A second stroke transverses three
More verticals. Our three score.

The right-angled tails like a semaphore,
Two bars that signal both the memory
Of so much you received and a sheer

Desire for a safe relay as we near
The crossing over. A smooth delivery.
A baton passed that passed before.

# Wood

### 1

This sign can hardly be misunderstood:
Trunks, crosstrees, the weeping shoots,
Three trees to token a forest or wood.

Stare at the middle then let the mind
Wander whichever path best suits,
So it chooses one, leaves two behind.

A dozen strokes conjure the unease,
Confusion of such different routes.
Here we see the wood for the trees.

### 2

On the edge and a little out of control:
Woodsman, hermit, partisan, rapparee
Flitting moss-footed behind some bole.

Nothing is quite as everything seems.
A track peters out, a futile vagary,
A path trailing off into our dreams

Of routes we once might have gone.
This path or that? Frost's quandary,
Promises you promised to deliver on.

### 3

Along the shafts of likelihoods
Down corridors of sun we drift,
At every fork still discerning

One way from another, learning
To arrive by whatever makeshift
Path, once we deliver the goods.

Never, never out of the woods.
A wanderlust. Compulsive gift.
Funnel of light in every yearning.

136

葉　HA

# Leaf

### 1

So intricate! Think with a stroke
Or two how easily you'd outline,
Say, the blade of maple or oak.

Instead to use tokens for 'growth',
'Era' and 'tree', so three combine
To muse on how a leaf is both

Generation and regeneration, a twin
Messenger, a sign and countersign
Of how things both fall and re-begin.

### 2

Vapour canals, a tissue of doors,
Thermostat, aperture, a steadfast
Network of veins, valve-like pores;

Some evergreen whatever transpires
Lasting as long as they need to last,
Or loose-leafed if their tree desires

As oaks, maples, sumacs or nervous
Aspens nailing their colours to the mast
While eras of leafage fall in service.

### 3

A leaf's blade with its *bl* sound
Waiting to blossom, to bloom, to blow.
Spans of foliage. Leafings and unleafings,

Unfolded ages of secreted briefings
On how to flourish. A gene flow
And code deciduously onward bound.

An age. A world. A cycle. A round.
An epoch of growth, another O
Curved in a bole's remembered springs.

言葉　KOTOBA

# Language

Utterance alongside a leaf
For 'language', 'word' or 'speech'.
Verbal blades, foliage of nouns,
A young bole branching out,
Small subtleties that ramify,
Twigging shade and nuance,
A whole vocabulary of tree
Unfolding its leafage.

From words' roots and stems,
A spring climbing and budding
To breathe in its leaves.

A burgeoning and tapping in.
Mirror world of branches:
One above uttering sunward,
Leaves expressing themselves;
The other one earthward, delving
The darker nourishments,
Keeping the grip, holding its ground.
Opening up. Burrowing below.

Sap quiver in leaves
Fluttering the tips of their tongue.
A flourishing word.

花  HANA

# Blossom

### 1

Firstly the cut-down version of two
Plants growing over a sign for change:
Twin Picasso figures, a side-view

Of someone standing up straight,
A second fallen; our human range
And span to say how flowers mutate.

*Like a flower of the field.* Upright.
Downfall. An image as lovely as strange.
A blossom revelling in its fragile light.

### 2

Year after year talk of *hanami*
'Blossom viewing'. No need to cite
Which tree as all over Japan

Friends are making contact to plan
To travel together. What week is right
To catch full bloom? Again to see

In clustered fists of a cherry tree
An aesthetic of all simple and quiet;
Petals flourishing their own lifespan.

### 3

In every such opening a fall begun,
No wonder within change the fright
Before unfurling towards the sun.

*Of course it hurts when buds break*
Unwombing what was safe and tight.
Everything gambled, all at stake.

Annual noiseless intensity of seeing
Fists of petals unclenching their light,
One shining out of spanless being.

花火　HANABI

# Fireworks

Fire-flower. Beside this, Germanic
Fireworks seem so earnest!
Chrysanthemum and dahlia shells
Burgeoning in the air,
Roman candles shooting their stars,
The blooms of Bengal lights,
Catherine wheels that spin and flourish,
Yellow, orange, green, red.

A Chinese cook's fluke?
Black powder. Chemical fire.
Bamboos detonate.

Roger Bacon the Franciscan
At Oxford feared the mix:
Charcoal, sulphur with saltpetre.
Where would gunpowder lead?
His coded findings hide for years
The shrapnel power behind
Peonies and weeping willows,
The fused cherry bomb.

Shush and hiss explode
Blossoming in the night sky.
A flower takes fire.

# Light

Variant of the sign for fire
Above a crouched human,
A bent figure bearing a torch,
Dark-breaker, light-bringer,
Yellow River luminary;
A signal beaconing
Someone's unbushelled light across
These five millennia.

A torch stroke by stroke
Scratched on an animal bone,
A signed tortoise shell.

Light that both reveals and blinds:
Too near, too dazzling,
Lucifer, lured by his brilliance,
Would fall so far from grace.
And yet this token still relayed,
Flambeau from hand to hand;
Light seen only by its own light,
Enough to show a way.

Stooped Olympian
Torch-bearer passing a flame,
A sign travels on.

神 KAMI

# God

Left a variant of altar
And right what was lightning,
A zigzag flash, a warning sign
Of high-voltage, unseen
Voice waggling from a telephone
Across a strip cartoon
But now brought into line can mean
'To state' or 'expound'.

Untamable jag.
In a bolt of forked lightning
A voice from beyond.

Thunder cloud's charged separation,
A sudden two-phased flash:
First glittering from cloud to earth,
Second stroke ground to cloud.
Heaven downwards and earth upwards,
Our jagged interplay;
In skies' jerky hieroglyphics
Signs of two-way traffic.

Altars conducting
Their skyline of least resistance.
A lightning grounded.

福 FUKU

# Luck

An altar appealing to gods
With a brimful wine jar
To bring down all gifts of well-being,
A drinking vessel blessed
By deities, mediation
Of 'good fortune' or 'luck',
A whole spectrum of 'happiness',
'Thriving', 'prosperity'.

Ancient wine-hued prayer:
That our cup will flow over.
*Demons out, luck in!*

History of humanity,
Leaking vessels we bring
To lay in hope on an altar,
Crying out for blessings.
Hallowed table and a full pot,
Pictogram and foretaste
Of a wedding feast at Cana
Three thousand years away.

Miraculous sign.
Our stone jars filled to their lips.
A divine vintage.

集　SHŪ

# Collection

Earlier three birds on a tree
But now only the one.
Imagine swoops of homing rooks
As evening tumbles in
Cawing and wheeling to gather
In skeleton branches
With nodes of old nests blackening
Into the roosting night.

Treetop colony.
A rookery congregates.
Dusky assemblage.

Whatever instinct makes us hoard,
A desire to amass,
Toys, dolls, marbles, bird's-nests and eggs
We fondle and brood on
Or how we'd swoop like rooks to nab
Spiky windfalls, stamping
Open their milky husks to touch,
Smooth marvels of chestnut.

The collector's dream
To feel, to caress, to keep.
A bird in the hand.

# Medium

Straight downward through a rectangle
A swift bisecting bar,
A stroke that likely started out
An arrow that pierces
Its target's: 'medium', 'mid-point', 'midst'.
Definite line between
Refocusing our edge-lured minds.
Golden mean. Middle way.

Shot and follow-through.
A true shaft and singing arc.
Spot on. A bull's-eye.

The sign too for Middle Kingdom.
A centered self-belief:
All else east or west of China.
Assured parishioners.
Poet Kavanagh would have approved
How any dynasty
Knew the axis of everything
Drew a line through their world.

The place where it's at.
Middle of everywhere.
Arrow's *you are here*.

集中　SHŪCHŪ

# Concentration

Collection at a middle point.
Mindful concentration
As our flights of fancy converge,
Vagaries homing in,
Ruffled feathers of distraction,
Flocks of unruly birds
Beating their wings around the bush
Now gather into one....

A rallied psyche
Nestles down. Zeroing in.
Density of thought.

*Statio* Benedict once named
The pause between two tasks;
A habit to break a habit,
An action brought to mind,
The moment we collect ourselves
In from the blurred edges.
Patience of filter and focus.
Screening out. Zooming in.

Bird perched and ready.
Concentred and gathered.
Our utmost presence.

# ADAGE

Proverbs are the product of daily experience

# Partings

*Partire è un po' mourire*
To part is to die a little

Even much younger I think I was aware
How in each departure a life has bled,
Another byte deleted in being's software,
A soul-leak, something of our essence shed.
No *forestalling dark with dark*, my friend,
As Herbert knew, love is love's true price
And each separation a trailer for an end,
Our meetings all foretastes of paradise.
Joke me again. I want to remember laughter
Yet each leave-taking now harder than before
As with the years stardust bones grow brittle;
Whatever heaven friendships hanker after
Every parting drains the marrow-bone.
*Every time we say goodbye, I die a little.*

*Mødes og skilles er livets gang, skilles og mødes er livets sang*
That we meet and part is life's way, that we part and meet life's song

All those encounters down through the years:
Chance meetings, ships passing in the night
Or once sweet sorrowed partings of Shakespeare's
Romeo, old flames long dropped out of sight.
Meetings and partings just the way things are,
No one could keep so many friendships in play,
Still some glimmer of desire in any *au revoir*
Never quite lets go that maybe some day...
Parting and meeting, a hope reversal implies:
*Arrivederci! auf Wiedersehen!* so long!
Even in our world that changes and drifts
This two-way saying that both accepts and lifts
With bittersweet undertones of a Danish folksong
The doubleness we hide in all goodbyes.

相 見 歡 笑 離 別 憂

*Xiāng jiàn huān xiào, lí bié yōu*
When meeting happy laughter, when parting grief

The deeper the delight at every re-meeting,
The deeper the transience running parallel;
Our leaving proportionate to our greeting,
Heywood's maxim *such welcome, such farewell.*
Hours of catching up, the days of fun
Relearning each other's common place,
Fluttered tongue of things done and undone,
Our kitchen conversation face to face.
And all those things we say we'll have to do,
Half-knowing how slyly time tiptoes
Already gone while we were only starting
But also more aware in every adieu
How in the light of endings friendship grows.
Laughter echoes even in the grief of parting.


*Ge cruaidh sgarachdainn, cha robh dithis gun dealachadh*
Though separation be hard, never did two meet but had to part

Severe reminder, a grave rhythm and tone,
In this Scottish proverb no hint of maybe,
More a warning that cuts so near the bone
Saying not just any two but you and me.
A meeting's joy forecasts an equal grief,
Yet Chinese and Italian allow us tomorrow,
In this stark sentence there's no reversal.
You not there for me nor me for you?
Even just at the thought a broken man.
Better that we don't know when or how.
*Though separation be hard never did two...*
I try to imagine what I know I never can,
Then turn again to now and now and now.

# Cheek

Teaching a fish to swim

We who came out of the sea,
We who so soon forget the womb
Hard put to relearn a buoyancy,
That fish out of water should presume
To do the business of those in the swim.
Cheek. The nerve. Such audacity!

*Eggið kennir hænunni að verpa*
The egg teaches the hen to lay eggs

Hen then egg or the order reversed,
For the old and wiser no backchat,
In Northern Europe hens came first.
A put-down for any young brat.
No doubts. Best seen and not heard.
A snub a proverb has long rehearsed.

*Les oisons veulent mener les ois paître*
The goslings want to drive the geese to pasture

The kind of cheek no goose should allow
After those weeks of broody caring,
But do geese play along as if somehow
They know youth is always overdaring?
No gosling would dare choose where to graze,
If goslings knew what geese know now.

*Teach your grandmother to suck eggs*

Did those grandmothers go robbing nests?
Why were they sucking them in any case?
Some secret skill these women possessed
To keep two generations in their place.
Whatever it was, don't teach your betters,
Whatever it was grandmothers knew best.

151

*Ag múnadh paidreacha don tsagart is iad ar fad aige féin*
Teaching prayers to the priest when he knows them all

Wings clipped if anyone dares
Advise those already in the know,
Echo of sharp-tongued forebears,
A double-edged counterblow,
A metaphor half-tongue-in-cheek:
As if you'd teach a priest his prayers!

釈迦に説法
*Shaka ni seppō*
Preaching to Buddha

Further east the meaning gene.
For Japanese losing the run
You preach to Buddha and intervene
Where best left to the serene one,
The Sage of Shakya. A young greenhorn
Upstaging the enlightened go-between.

不要 班 門 弄 斧
*Bù yào Bán mén nòng fǔ*
Don't fool around Ban's gate with an axe

A bungler with axe creating a mess,
Some apprentice hopeless effrontery
Determined willy-nilly to impress
Ban Jiang the god of carpentry.
The high sign. A word to the wise.
Wink tipped in transcendent playfulness.

152

# Moving On

It's no use crying over spilt milk

Over the world this Sophocles cry
As spilt fluid seeps into clay;
Leaking vessels, a kicked bucket,
Lost milk of our human regret,
Liquid that never returns to its tray.

*Ce qui est fait est fait*
What is done is done

You can almost hear a Joblike sigh.
French or German or Scandinavian:
The happened can't be made unhappen.
Plain matter of fact. No metaphor.
A mistake it's better to ignore.

*Aqua pasada no mueve molino*
Water gone by doesn't move a mill

In Spain water, in Holland wind,
What's downstream drives no wheel,
Scruples never moved a sail
To turn the mill and grind to meal,
Flow and whim of all we bewail.

*Níl maith sa seanchas nuair atá an anachain déanta*
Talk is no good when the harm is done

Sure if only I'd known in time...
All our *ifs* and *ands* but still
Hedging a field already ruined,
Hindsighted babble of goodwill
Binding up another's wound.

*Rhy hwyr codi pais ar ôl piso*
Too late to lift a petticoat after pissing

Under our tears an earthy humour.
A self-deprecating Welsh laughter
Or Japan's 'tightening buttocks after
Breaking wind'. O smile Rabelais!
All our thoughts still housed in clay.


Слезами горю не поможешь
Tears don't help trouble

Treeless steppes too harsh for weeping
And an old Cossack within who fears
How clogged self-pity nurtures sloth.
No sobbing. Yet the salt of tears.
Cries and waterings of inner growth.


落花枝に帰らず、破鏡再び照らさず
*Rakka eda ni kaerazu, hakyō hutatabi terasazu*
Fallen blossoms don't return to branches, a broken mirror doesn't
  reflect again

A Japanese child mourns blossoms.
A glass once whole, a leafy bough.
Margaret knows what Hopkins meant
When fallen years of mirror fragment.
Memory is then. Life is now.


*Aldrei skal gráta gengna stund*
Never cry for time gone

Saga of a stable's bolted horse,
Spilt milk and fallen leaves,
Broken mirror and the wind gone.
We cry for what nothing retrieves.
In our weeping we move on.

# Unsaid

Toute vérité n'est pas bonne à dire
Every truth is not the right thing to say

Something French and human here:
Thought first filtered through the head,
Gossip others shouldn't know
Things we'd better leave unsaid.
Poised, forgiving, shrewd, urbane,
Why a fuss when there's no gain?
Rise above it unconcerned,
Best not known, a blind-eye turned –
Almost careless *bonne à dire.*

Truth is truth. The truth alone.
Fraud unveiled, the trails we'd blaze,
World we'd change, a world our own,
Endless talking student days,
Hard-nosed, certain, fact's a fact,
Age has ripened years of tact.
Subtler now than our first flush,
Sometimes speak and sometimes hush.
Truth is also time and tone.

Friendship's silent idiom
Prudent as a diplomat
Knowing when the word's mum.
Much unsaid but hinted at,
Half in earnest, half jocose
Understood between the close,
All you know you'll never say,
Secrets brought alone to clay,
Songs best sung by singing dumb.

*Sanningen är bland det finaste vi har, den skal vi passa på att inte bruka i otid*
Truth is one of the finest things we have, we need to watch out not to use it at the wrong time

A slow rambling Swedish byword.
Someone in low October light
Repeats old prudence.

Who had blurted a confidence
Or some fact when the time was wrong
So all was misheard?

Precept of tact and etiquette:
Proverb's singsong drawl
Finest, nevertheless,

Truth's still truth if told with finesse,
Knowing what's both best to recall
And best to forget.


言わぬは言うにまさる
*Iwanu wa iu ni masaru*
Non-saying outdoes saying

Come day, go day, ebb and flow,
Just that gaze and still we know

Deep within our unsaid zone
What's unuttered each has known,

One caressing look can glean
All the years of might-have-been

Time now noiselessly atones.
Still as Kyōto's garden stones

Passion's silent interplay,
Eyes that speak what tongues can't say.

# Accommodation

柳に風
*Yanagi ni kaze*
In a willow, wind

Young and full of hungry sap
No one could really understand
Why that pussy willowing,
Weeping while it's billowing,
Flexing as the winds expand
Limbs that dance and overlap,
Boughs that sway but never snap,
Bend, caress and yet withstand.

Better then to bow than break.
Shaking trees are last to fall.
Words that once seemed so fake,
'Bend' like 'bow' had meant to crawl;
Words for fogeys, words for clones,
Old too young and no backbones,
Wily, streetwise, on the make.

Many things we'd thought we'd do.
Time for youth and time to rage,
Time to learn to court a breeze,
Bending with her lure and tease
Root and settle stage by stage.
Wisdom comes when wisdom's due.
Cake that's kept and eaten too,
Reckless youth and rueless age.

Drifting leaves flirt and sough,
Swirl the wind on steady roots
Shaping futures in each bough,
Cricket bats and sallow flutes,
Cradle boards to crib a daughter.
Dipping low to kiss the water,
Knowing geishas take their bow.

*Vannet vet mer enn oss, det finner alltid letteste vei*
Water knows more than us, it always finds the easiest way

Can you hear Grieg's *Spring* beginning to spill?
Crusted snow
Or ice-floe
Tinkle by tinkle gathering its thaw
Into a rill
That feeds a rush and swirl of water.

Anywhere there's water, there's a way
To go
With a flow
Carving and smoothing its river-bed,
Cantabile,
Oozing around molehills and mountains.

Liquid grace, serial u-turner,
Arpeggio
Of H$_2$O
That leaps and swerves or changes course,
Curved learner
Shaping and shaped in how it is.


Better to bend the neck than to bruise the forehead

A bowing willow
Or rush and seep of water
But near the bone
Thumps on the front of the skull
Rattling stars in the brain-box.

A medieval house
With a lower stone lintel,
A tall youngster fails
To stoop. A dazed cranium.
A bruise on the memory.

Unbending young man
Banging his head against walls,

Stiff-necked ne'er-do-well
Upsetting portal-keepers
Watching thresholds they can't pass.

If only you'd known.
No need to be a doormat,
Bow and straighten up.
Always a new-brooming youth!
Is this an older man's song?

# Confusion

*Too many cooks spoil the broth*

Who are these cooks? What are they up to?
These broth-makers who keep showing up
And spoiling the kitchens with their brew.

One says a soupçon, another says a cup –
No Indians, everyone the chef in chief –
A third is now pouring one extra sup.

More seasoning. Just another bayleaf.
Were they mischievous then or genuine?
Scandanavia and Italy the same motif.

A spicey tale from Greek or Latin
On through Germany to Budapest?
A boy I imagined salt ladled in

Heap after heap and a droughty guest,
Then how in its telling the gossip grew,
A proverb travelling north and west.

船頭多くして、舟山に登る
*Sendō ōku shite, fune yama ni noboru*
Skippers increase and the boat climbs a mountain

For French two bosses,
Many steer in Welsh,
In Greek surplus advisers.

Too many skippers,
A boat noses down
To Davy Jones's locker.

But not in Japan.
Here in the scramble
Sailors trip each other up,

Command, countermand,
Topsyturvy world,
Torn masts and a bow ascends

Surreal Mount Fuji;
Nightmare of seascape
Where the boat climbs a mountain.

У семи́ ня́нек дитя́ без гла́зу
*U semi nyanek ditya bez glazu*
With seven nurses, a child without an eye

East in Europe too many midwives
Spoiling all those deliveries,
But by the time the saying arrives
In Russia it's nurses or nannies

Busy fussing over this and that,
Cross-purposed madams who fly
At each other or absorbed in chat
Fail to keep their weather eye

On an infant now half out of sight
And minds preoccupied with scandal,
The juice and gossip of last night,
Leaving each other a chance to dandle

A child but never quite sure why
It crawled so near a dangerous drop.
Seven nurses. No watchful eye.
Who knows where the buck must stop?

*Vielen Hirten, übel gehütet*
Many shepherds, ill-protected

Right across the ancient Near East
Gods or kings as wise or humble shepherd,
Tender of frail and wayward,
Staff and crook
And priest.
A sadder dictum than sailor, nanny or cook.

161

Seasoned bonds of nomad sheep and keeper,
The injured carried, the thief warded off,
Daily gathering at the trough
Or watering-hole,
The deeper
Their rapport, the steeper now a sudden fall.

What happened once on a German hillside?
Too many shepherds confused or too blasé
To fetch a blundering stray?
A flock nonplussed,
As wall-eyed
Sheep plunge abysses of broken trust.


       *Obra de común, obra de ningún*
       A work in common, no one's work

Such strange geographies,
Networks of adage,
Nurse, shepherd, cook or sailor.

But was this once tried?
Line by line by line
Quixotic subcommittee

In monthly meetings
Squabbling out a book,
Sancho Panza consensus

Reducing those giants
To windmills, their arms
Wind-sails to turn the millstones

Grinding to a halt
Our common yearning
Solo dreamers represent.

*Hummingbird of love.*
Lone can-carrier.
*Sí, aquí.* The buck stops here.

# Praise

*Mol an óige agus tiocfaidh sí*
Praise youth and it will prosper

A youngster's smile climbed from the root
Of his being, a blossom so suddenly sprung,
Out of such clay one burgeoning offshoot.

I'd forgotten a friend's father's razor tongue
And how in turn he couldn't praise his son.
A memory stinging again as it was stung.

Everything in him wanted to say 'well done!
'Good on you, my boy! That was flawless!'
No fault to find but why was there always one

To hamper delight he so wanted to express?
For the one stunted tree, an unseen wood.
Too long a longing for his own father's caress.

A friend's son I'd praised in all likelihood
By chance, a small thing I happened to salute
But my words sank deeper than I'd understood.

Down silent wells of generations a chute
Of praise moistened years of childhoods unsung;
A shaft of sap pushing upwards to the fruit.

*Sannarlegt lof er ekki um of*
Real praise isn't about excess

Nothing on islands of glaciers and volcanoes
Allows for flattery or soft-soaped excess.

No school of blurb and puff or false kudos,
Feelgood factor, success to easy success.

Over the windswept lava a sober tending,
A weighing up. And even so the overflow.

Geysers of warmth, Hekla's cup sending
Again from middle-earth a molten glow,

A crimson boost of praise somehow starker
Against bleak landscapes, as the sudden delight

Of an old teacher brandishing a new marker
To underline in red everything that's right.


Old praise dies unlesse you feede it.

An outlandish proverb Herbert knew,
Long fallen by the wayside;
Instead a hawk-eyed
'Giving credit where credit is due'.

Tame worthiness. No splurge of belief
In an overflowing cup.
A root dies up.
A withered branch, a fallen leaf.

Flare and blaze. The first whirl-about
Of Solomon's poured song,
But unoiled too long
A bridegroom's lamp sputters out.

Teachers in whose inner light we'd grown,
A daily laid hand,
All flaws in sand,
Our wonders etched in red stone.

A mentor's feeding words, a lover's gaze,
Water's lavish spill;
And are we still
Each other's *secretarie of praise*?

# Waitings

*Þeir fá byr sem bíða*
Those who wait get a fair wind

A drift of sailors leagues south of Reykjavík
Becalmed and calmly choosing to sit it out
Or maybe even caught in freak
Storms that darken from the north,
Tightening up to go about.

Endless hours of beating, switched tack.
Somehow from these words trust inferred
That out of the blue winds back,
Sails bellying on a beam reach,
Again their bow nosing home.

Whoever makes time has eons up a sleeve.
And so both to abandon and anticipate
In gaining little to achieve
A handing over, a self-surrender.
Is there all the time in the world to wait?

果報は寝て待て
*Kahō wa nete mate*
Sleep and wait for good fortune

Go and sleep on it!
Do I hear a monk's
Voice in a Kyōto temple

Or a local lord
A shōgun baron
Counselling his samurai

To puzzle deeply,
Or try to work out
Everything as best he can

And then to let go?
With time and patience
A mulberry bush becomes

A silk kimono.
Unravel in sleep
All sleep ravels up again.


*Tout vient à point à qui sait attendre*
All things come as needed to those who know how to wait

So much doing in our waiting.
Milton serving his light denied,

A Zen master contemplating
Worlds of action turning inside.

The lover who begins as doer
Declaring his hand never knows,

A passive, time-biding wooer
Becalmed until the spirit blows.

The muse resisting any rush,
A scribbler readying at her call,

Around and round a mulberry bush
Tending till the tongues may fall.

# Shortfall

*Einmal ist keinmal*
Once is not at all

For beginners a heartening motto:
*Einmal ist keinmal*, once won't hurt,
At least give everything one go.

That girl in Hamburg afraid to fall
And her father lifting her into the saddle,
'Come on, once isn't once at all'.

Trusting in motion and a bike's panache,
She shrieks and thrills but losing nerve
Fräulein's wobbles a sideways crash.

And now a soothing tantamount
To saying 'a first try is written off',
*Einmal ist keinmal*, once doesn't count.

A proverb to brace the faint of heart
And bolster shortfalls in advance;
Our failures forgiven before we start.


*Tann sum tíðum rør út, hann fiskar umsíðir*
The one who often rows out, catches fish in the end

Backbone. Long-haul grit.
Fishermen oaring
Bravely out from the Faroes

And day after day
Facing a knife-edge,
The cliffhangers of failure,

Chance of tides and shoals,
Skill, hunch and hearsay,
Rowing unforgiving seas.

Again and again,
Belief in frequence,
The gleam of tomorrow's catch.

七転び八起き
*Nana korobi ya oki*
Seven stumbles, eight getting ups

A child learning to ride
Or maybe a sumō apprentice falling
By the ringside?

Again the trawl and line
Laid to trap a moment's wonder,
A trace, a sign,

A perfect mix of thought
And feeling, something wrestled with
And surely caught.

Just as I've written *stet*
The proof of a moment has fled,
Slipped the net.

Tomorrow is keeping faith.
Seven seas. Seven veils. Seven falls.
But, then, the eighth!

# Falling

*Gutta cavat lapidem non vi sed saepe cadendo*
The drop hollows the stone not by force but by often falling

Ovid's droplet on a stone,
A signet ring grown thin,
A plough worn down by soft clay.

The trickle most widely known,
For some a motto to underpin
Where there is a will there is a way.

Persistence. For me an undertone
Of danger. My mother in the kitchen
Warning as we went out to play

'Constant dripping wears a stone'.
Any bad company that we were in
Would whittle and whittle us away.

A ring worn near to the bone,
Ovid's epistle under the skin.
I hear you mother and I obey.


*Liten tue velter stort lass*
A clump of earth overturns a large load

Ovid took his drip-worn stone from Greek
But here a cart is rattling along fjords

On narrow rutted lanes or winding towards
A forest clearing watching for any freak

Clump or tuft that might upend its freight.
Again the championing of what's small

Or riding a boastful flaw before his fall,
Proud Agamemnon in a low northern light.

朱に交われば赤くなる

*Shu ni majiwareba, akaku naru*
If you mix with vermilion, you become red

No beat about bush
Or softening clay,
This Japanese straight talking

Allowed in proverbs,
An admonishment
Mother would have understood.

It might be the poured
Voice of Sirach's son
'He that toucheth pitch...'

Who lies down with dogs
Will rise up with fleas.
Earthy images that warn.

But caught red-handed?
Vermilion smeared.
Indelible crimson stain.

# Upstream

*Hva∂ ungur nemur, gamall temur*
Young should learn if old should know how

Green time of learning
When young we acquired
Knowledge for our doyen days.

Pliant years a mind
Mimicked and sifted
Skills it stowed unconsciously,

But also a sense
How ease and know-how
Travel those generations,

Young to old to young,
Mastered, handed on
Saga of a thousand years,

Current of learning,
Craft riding the flow
Young should learn if old should know.

學如逆水行舟，不進則退
*Xué rú nì shuǐ xíng zhōu, bù jìn zé tuì*
Learning is like rowing upstream, not to advance is to fall back

Is to live to learn,
Thrill-seeking headway,
Our bending, our stretch, our gain?

Rowing the Yangtse
Someone knew the kick
In the tempo of a stroke,

Surge of hard-won ground,
A fraction of all
We know we can never know

Earned against the flow.
There's no rowing back,
Any resting on our oars.

Catch and pull and drive,
Rhythms of learning.
A blade glints in the water.


*Caiff dyn dysg o'i grud i'w fedd*
A human learns from cradle to grave

Span of our passage
From eye openings,
And gurglings in the crib's boat.

Two forgotten years
Of absorption – more
Than the whole rest of a life.

A long learning curve
Flattens and stretches
Over ripening decades.

Slow, sweeter strivings,
*Aha!* of the new
Looming beyond another bend.

Old dog and new tricks;
Livelong making ready,
Striving upstream to the source.

# Poise

上手の手から水が漏る
*Jōsu no te kara mizu ga moru*
Out of skilful hands water leaks

Tight-butted palms with fingers crooked
To scoop water up;
Between the cup and the lip,
A tale of seepage.

So everything attained seems fluked,
Hurried sip and sup,
A cribbed lucky dip,
Digital slippage.

Let off by proverb. Unhooked.
Pardon our clay cup
Its cracks and gaps that drip.
Human leakage.


*D'er inkje tre så reint, det ei har ein kvist*
There's no wood so perfect, it doesn't have a knot

Our time seemed a time of perfect wood,
History's final advance.
*I was green in judgment, cold in blood.*

God be with the callow days of youth,
Salad days of arrogance,
Sapling dreams of simpler knotless truth.

Year by year loppings of unripe pride.
Pruned back to tolerance,
Trees still earning axioms from inside.

An unforgiven self is a kind of paralysis,
A closing down on chance,
We relearn 'a good marksman can miss'.

For the naïve all but themselves were naïve.
Sap fresh in ascendance,
Has every young man a fool in his sleeve?


*Ní bhíonn saoi gan locht*
No sage is flawless

So many ways to say this:
Monkeys too fall from trees,
Horses with four legs can tumble
And an old woman may blunder.

A smiled compassion. Horace's
'Even Homer nods'. The ease
With which we forgive a stumble.
We're not our mistakes and under

Any guise, leak or marksman's miss,
Message the same in all of these:
At once human, wise and humble,
The poise and not the flaw our wonder.

# Once-off

光陰、矢のごとし
*Kōin, ya no gotoshi*
Light-shadow, like an arrow

A bowstring's taut
Kick and sudden let-go
Pent up energy
To flee and flee,
Our one-way arrow.

Flight of time caught
In a Japanese compound noun:
Light and shadow,
*Chiaroscuro*
Of sun-up, sundown.

*Sola kjem att men same dagen kjem ikkje*
The sun comes back but the same day doesn't.

Think of January in Norway.
Infinities of snow,
A watched pot slow
Thaw of dark towards spring.

Then, imagine a July day
And half-bright night,
As summer's sleight
Of hand draws in its evening.

Fireball of come day go day
Even in its backslide
Seems steady beside
The human arc, an arrow's whizz.

The sun shines. Make hay.
A once-off glow
In light or shadow.
Take time as time is.

175

Someone hurries across the strand
To launch before the high and dry.
The moon's taut bow can't wait.

Mother falters on Douglas beach.
Maybe the afternoon. Late, too late,
The crest has fallen, the sun gone.

Time and tide merge into one
As they recede. So easy to hesitate.
Hair's-breadth moment to wade in.

The waves ebb and underlap.
To stand outside grieving fate
Or plunge into the swim of things?

Time is water and water runs.
Light or shadow. Still to celebrate.
To embrace the flux. To ride the swell.

# Mindful

*La reconnaissance est la mémoire du cœur*
Gratitude is the memory of the heart

A warning menu of forgotten bread
And man's ingratitude. A dearth
Of trust. But this French saying?

Stone-eared and dumb from birth,
A boy at Semens refused
Schooling learns from an Abbé in Paris.

What is gratitude? his teacher mused
And deaf-mute Massieu wrote
'Gratitude is *la mémoire du coeur.*'

A soundless byte spreads as a quote,
Blurs into proverb.
An answer stowed in human memory.

飲水思源
*Yǐn shuǐ sǐ yuán*
If you drink from the stream, remember the spring

Hunkering low on a bank
To cup handfuls of water,
Where to begin to thank?

Yellow River of a gene
Received, down-draft
Of words passed between

Generations, slow nurture
Of groves holding earth,
Allowing a scoop and curvature,

A brook's scrape and groove,
Communities that nourished,
Gradual shapings of love.

Sudden opened floodgate.
Unstoppable onrush of thanks.
The heart-memory in spate.

This stream takes up everything.
One sweet water.
Drink from a remembered spring.

# Calling

*Ní féidir leis an ngobadán an dá thrá a fhreastal*
A sandpiper cannot tend two shores

Yes, of course, Kierkegaard was right:
Purity of heart is to love one thing.

For twenty helter-skelter years a niggling
Of too little done before the gentle night.

Brown-backed white-bellied wader
Teetering hurriedly between two shores.

Too tired after those day-job chores;
A muse's overwhelmed serenader.

Then the gift and scope of another score
To wade wherever a tidal rip demands.

A bobbing, nodding head in the sands.
A sandpiper busy on a single shore.


If you run after two hares, you will catch neither

My father's whispering I recall
*Pity too damned intense, too hyper,*
*Hunting every hare he can.*

On our island once the sandpiper.
But across a landmass to Japan
*Deux lièvres, zwei Hasen, Nito.*

Lesson one for any huntsman.
Only a fool would ever go
Running after two hares at once.

This easy smiling *bon mot*
Of knowing fathers warning sons
How quickly hares go to ground.

Dream-chaser I stick to my guns,
Run with hare, hunt with hound.
O no, *mon père,* I'll catch them all.


*En kan ikke ri to hester samtidig*
(One cannot ride two horses at one time)

To travel overland to Trondheim
Or bring good news
From Ghent one horse at a time.

But yes that red-bloused circus rider
Astride two horses
Reining the gap when it spilt wider

Over the haltered here and there
Applause endorses
Between the saddle and the giddy air

And fallen for the wonder of a ring
I couldn't choose
Either the moment or its beckoning

When rein and rhythm correspond
In sway and rhyme.
Sweet here. Sweet beyond.

# Ease

能ある鷹は爪を隠す
*Nō aru taka wa tsume o kakusu*
A gifted hawk hides its talons

An air of cunning? A cute hawk
Tucking away its claws
To stalk
Some unsuspecting prey?

But in Japan this is how to say
Gifted have no need
To display
Their wares or flaunt a skill.

Shakespeare's *power to hurt and will*
*Do none.* The sharpest talons
And still
Hawks lie down with doves.


*An dias is troime,'sí is ísle ceann*
The heaviest ear of corn bows lowest

I imagine Dvořák's Bohemian tune
Swaying its *largo* in ears of corn
And over horizons of longing,
A New World
Slowly unfurled
Through miles of ripening meadow.

A melody both childlike and endless
Swells in the ears. Yearning beyond
Yearning. A hawk rides
The breeze.
Infinite ease
Of knowing how little I know.

Sunlight hoarded in nodding corn.
Humble hearts, humble desires.
A confidence rich and weighty
*Defeatable*
*By means of the beatable.*
Surety of bending low.

# Shades

*Ar scáth a chéile a mhaireas na daoine*
People live in each other's shade

Here figures walking
Ahead in downpours
Sheltering others behind.

Our way of saying
Two footsteps no path,
One tree can't make a forest.

German *Heute mir,*
*Morgen dir* reminds
Me today, you tomorrow.

My shade, your shadow.
Zulu's down-to-earth
'One hand washes another

'And both will be clean'
Rubbing together
A mutual becoming.

前人種樹，後人乘涼
*Qián rén zhòng shù, hòu rén chéng liáng*
One generation plants, another gets the shade

We live in each other's shade
And walk a middle land
Between what was and will be.

Millennia of China expand
A proverb's reach. Shadow relayed
Age to age. A care's extensity.

The signs for before and after,
People, seed, tree and shade;
Limbs stretching out of our past.

A debt prepaid and post-paid.
Plan-receiver, plan-draughter.
A shade taken, a shadow cast.

# Abandon

*Den tid, den sorg*
That time, that sorrow.

So much caution before you've begun
Insisting you look before you leap,

Reminding you to walk before you run,
How the one you love, makes you weep.

But this loophole a let-off and let-go,
A sort of polar grandfather clause.

A spring to sow, a summer to reap
As dragonflies stretch wings of gauze.

High jinks under a midnight sun.
No darkness now and no tomorrow.

Of all our moments this the one.
Hell, high water. That time, that sorrow.


*Kümmere dich nicht um ungelegte Eier*
Do not worry about eggs not yet laid

Frettings over a morning's eggs?
Further south temperate
Troubles, a tamer climate
Fevers of midnight sun outstrip.

Such a sober letting rip,
Longheaded ecstasy,
Careful strategy
Of crossing only bridges we meet.

*Let the morn come with its meat.*
An abandon only halfway
Sufficient unto the day;
Tomorrow lurks in the heat of now.

明日は、明日の風が吹く
*Ashita wa, ashita no kaze ga fuku*
As for tomorrow, tomorrow's wind blows

For the Japanese
Moments we borrow,
Time's arrow on loan for fun.

And so no unease,
No bridge or sorrow,
Sheer lightness of abandon.

Quivers of a breeze
Put off tomorrow,
Trusting to the rising sun.

# GRATITUDE

Thou hast giv'n so much to me,
Give one thing more, a gratefull heart.

GEORGE HERBERT

# Blaenau Ffestiniog

### 1

Days of echoed chats. Roberts y Post,
Wil Tattos the potato van man,
Endless teas with dark haired Mrs Pryce;
I'm nineteen here in Tan y Grisiau
Housed with twice widowed Mrs Lewis.

At first nervous of her young lodger –
Paddies had built a local power plant
One fine morning she'd found a navvy
Sleeping it off in her garden shed –
Yet I'd thought she'd begun to settle.

Question by question I gather words
But she hears her second husband's voice
Stumbling and childish after his stroke.
At breakfast pills scattered the table,
My hostess can take no more of me.

Her parting peace offering one husband's
Spurrell's Welsh-English dictionary
Signed August 4th 1966,
Mari Lewis. Demurring mother,
Your dismissed son still remembers you.

### 2

Like Seth I've fallen on my feet.
Mr and Mrs Owens my foster pair
Who'd lost a son and now find me.
A semi by the end of a terraced street
Jutting off Blaenau Ffestiniog's Square
Out over the lip of a river valley.

12 Bryn Bowydd my Welsh berth.
Mr Owens, chapel elder and slate cutter,
Tireless after a day at his dressing mill
Pours his tea and talks for all he's worth
Between his hunks of bread and butter.
*Dwy galon*, he laughs, Two-hearted Phil.

Doris birdlike, good to her marrow,
A country girl from Cwm Nantcol,
She'd fallen for her talking Blaenau beau;
Downright and dutiful house sparrow
She loved to break her daily protocol
With Sunday drives to Chester or Llandudno.

Forty years older a Christmas bulletin
In her headline copy script to say
*Ma' Phil wedi marw*, out of his pain,
Over ninety his second heart given out.
My mind clouds a 'Stiniog day,
Bryn Bowydd is veiled in slaty rain.

3

Let the resurrection siren sound,
Blink us forth from dusty caverns
Dazzled and gladly over ground
By chapels and diehard taverns
Back through the dove-grey light
Cast from slated streets and waste
Past the Co-'p and Square, then right,
Homeward now the ashen-faced.

Loyal to your prince and crown
Beware hot-headed Papist schemes;
Old Lloyd George's Whiggish town,
No foolishness or 'Welsh Nash' dreams.
Wonder and ask could this be true,
Picture cards from Dublin show a bus?
Sundays at least a chapel or two.
'You see he's speaking just like us!'

4

I don't think R.S. Thomas liked his flock,
Neither Evans nor Prytherch nor Job Davies,
*Uneasy fossil in the mind's rock*
He feared them all as Kavanagh feared Maguire –
*A gofid gwerin gyfan*
*Yn fy nghri fel taerni tân* –
A people's grief my cry's nagging fire.

The grey cramped womb of Blaenau Ffestiniog,
Crimean Pass of Merionethshire,
Cradles memories of dusty fog
Swirling in beams of a slate miner's lantern.
Dai Du gives a mate a lash,
Jim Bach's a 'Welsh Nash'.
*Pesychu* 'to cough' an important word to learn

When stooping over rubble wagons with grease.
*Eisiau seim!* We push them round the jagged bends.
In Blaenau Square they sit and wheeze,
The grinder's disease will have them hook or crook.
*I'll go with you and be your guide*
*In thy most need to go by your side*
Postman Pierce reads his Everyman book.

Poor R.S. struggling with his own kind.
For me only their warmth and wake through time
Etched against the slate waste tips they'd mined.
O pit-ponies Dai and Jim and Aled
Stoop to smear the wagon creaking
Noise of small hearts breaking.
I bless a town that gave me all it had.

# Homeland

### 1

Age of open heart and talking soul,
Feverish plans of callow time out,
Suspended time of sixty-eighters

Before the routines of survival,
Our habits of settled common sense,
This aperture for livelong friendships.

Oslo of snow-boots and *Pils* and trams,
City of youth and orphan stumblings
I grew up here with sibling students.

All hail those who made me one of you,
You who let me strike these other roots;
I flourish in my second homeland.

### 2

Bjørn, my proto-Scandanavian,
Long-legged, blond and blue-eyed gleam of charm,
Dreamy mountaineer those years adrift,
Mix of make belief and action man.

'Noble the human, the earth is rich'
Mood by mood our nightly poems aloud,
*Edelt er mennesket, jorden er rik*
Nordahl Grieg's *To Youth* at fever pitch.

'Dance my lyric, weep my song'
Skjæraasen and Herman Wildenvey
'Life's desire so strong and near and new'
*Danse mi vise, gråte min sang.*

Me a poet, you now glacialist,
Every time we meet in two score years,
Quoting Gunnar's words you'd quoted me,
Ghostly Rudin I once more insist:

'Don't forget the one you've never met,
She's the one you love in her you love'
Action man remember now your dream?
Lines of mine move daily in your debt.

3

Gratitude's language.
For food. For today. For now.
A tongue to thank in.

# Edda

### 1

A fling that ends as quickly as it started
But I'm among Oslo's Iceland crowd;
A few doubtful but mostly open-hearted,
Half-curious about this *Íri*, half-proud.
'Black Death' or beer our nights on the tear,
Sundays Hallgrímur puts me through my paces;
You clearheaded, me the worse for wear,
Busy trying to parse those Eddic phrases.
*Maðr er mannz gaman.* 'Man's joy man'.
A world cut stone by stone that undergirds
Each noun's monochrome Germanic freight,
A tongue like Hopkins' favoured Anglo-Saxon,
Tee-aitches, *eð*'s, its saga-ness of words
Nearer now than English to Alf the Great.

### 2

Could I have had a better guide,
Hallgrímur, Magnús góði's son
Who'd over generations taught
Reykjavík's pupils to decline?

*En gaman!* And all the more fun!
You tell how the skaldic kenning,
A playful and roundabout phrase,
Now too can mean 'a theory'.

Most of all that sense of delight,
Gift of joy. With Laxness we say:
*Ég fékk hann til láns af láni*
I got as a loan of a loan...

'Often liking with little won,
With loaf half cut, with cup half drained'
A sharp-eyed love of what's simple.
'I find myself a fellow soul.'

**3**

Two generations on we sit
On a sunny Donnybrook wall
Talking over Gödel's *kenning*.
'Tell me All-Wise thou knowest all?'
'Such my wiles that they seek in vain.'

Our saga unfolds its wisdom.
'Before young, I'd fared all alone.
Then I'd drifted. I know how rich
I struck it, finding another.
*Maðr er mannz gaman.* Man's joy man.'

# Barcelona

### 1

Strolling la Rambla de les Flors,
Sometimes, Spanish, sometimes Catalan.
Franco still can rule his stubborn roost.

1970 and Raimon sings:
*Buscant a Déu, al vent de món*
'Seeking God, the wind of our world'.

Pablo land, Cassells and Picasso too.
Soon as Montserrat unlocked her door
Here I knew at once I'd struck it rich.

Swarthy, ageless, wealthy draper's wife,
Open-faced, so warm and charged with fun.
Daughter Concha tutored me at home.

Mother like the first who mothered me
Offering now her gifts of praise and tongue.
Yes! Aixó mateig! Exactly so!

Slowly born I'm growing here again.
*I ja le nèixer és un gran plor*
'And our birth already one great cry'.

### 2

Barcelona days you nourish me,
Rôle to which you easily revert.
Would this fit I wonder? *Creg que si*
Sending home a leather miniskirt.
All those *v*'s pronounced as if they're *b*'s
*J*'s and *s*'s don't rub the mouth,
Arabs didn't reach as far as these,
Lisps and gutturals still further south.
No flamenco or fiery castanet,
Port of trade and merchant middleman,
Stately as a slow sardana dance,
Brittle Spanish light and somehow yet
Here's this straddling world of Catalan,
Halfway house between Castile and France.

3

Sunday it's a climb to Montserrat.
There an open square for us to dance;
Brass, woodwind and drum the *combla* plays
6/8 rhythm sardanas in the sun,
Down-toned klezmer weaves us in.

Named from this serrated pilgrim mount
You're enfolded in that plaza's dance.
Tambourine and bass proclaim *mercès!*
*Gràcies! Montserrat Castells,*
*La meva mama catalana.*

# Deutsch

## 1 *Frau*

*Ach du lieber Gott!* I learn to say,
Words first heard in dingy Dublin rooms
Chatting hours with *Frau* in exile Smith,
Half flirtatious pouring out her past:
Three times wed and now this third time stuck,
Living here for daughter Hildegard.
*Ach*, she sighs each time she speaks of 'him'.
Once a dancer. Look my photograph!
*Aber* men no longer double-take.

Say now where all the men are gone.
*Ach ja, sag mir, wo die Männer sind.*
Always such long-distance happiness,
Here nostalgic, there dissatisfied.
Giving in I slowly draw away.
Then I hear that she's returning there –
Could I maybe even wish her well?
Saddest nurturer I'd ever had.
Unforgiven, still this need for thanks.

## 2 *Rhythm*

Why I love this *Deutsch* it's hard to say.
Downrightness, some hold on clarity,
German parts I somehow want to play?
Earnest *Doppelgänger* sleep in me?
Concepts seem to grow so sure and clear,
Stark as each staccato idiom,
Doubts or qualms now somehow disappear
Warding off each argument's *warum?*
Loops of iambs persuade now even me –
*Raffiniert* 'refined' can now mean 'sly' –
*Alles muss so klar und deutlich sein!*
Plain and straight as everything must be.
Wait and wait the sense comes by and by –
Verbs kept back like Cana's finest wine.

## 3  *Pfeils*

Strange the hoops of chance that took me here:
*Geschwister-Scholl-Straße*, Alpirsbach,
Street that's named for student siblings Scholl,
White Rose pamphleteers the Nazis killed,
Apt address for such attentive friends,
Close and open how they welcome me!
Pfeils the gentlest pair I think I've met;
I'm at home and spread my German wings.

Teach me *heute mir* and *morgen dir*
Turned around becomes compassion's core:
'All that's yours today, tomorrow's mine.
Bach's St Matthew and Rilke's Elegies,
Dietrich's *Wann wird man je verstehn?*
*Mein Gott!* 'When will we ever understand?'
Here the Germany I'll always love.
Pitch my *Heimat* tent at Alpirsbach.

# Poitiers

### 1

For weeks at Poitiers a widow takes me in.
Her husband, then her daughter dead from grief,
Josy Montaigne, proud of Spanish origin
Somehow hangs by threads of her belief.
A life unfurling I attend all ears,
Her memory by memory recall,
We talk and talk unburdening it all
Till slowly an older *joie de vivre* grows.
Chansons. I'm taught Piaf and Barbara:
'When he takes me in his arms,' she sings,
Reminded moments of her *Vie en Rose*,
*Quand il me prend dans ses bras...*
A touch of joy in Poitiers' late spring.


### 2

Rev. J.A. Moran SM's
French Grammar and Composition:
No slurred words or syllables
Action of the organs of speech
More vigorous, sharp, than English...
O school *Français!*

All those pursed up haughty vowels,
The huffs and puffs of sullen lips,
Such shrugged shoulders and open palms,
Pouting, sulky, nasal, sultry,
How every word caresses me.
O moody *Français!*

Not just sorry but *désolé*
Or to stop at thanks a million
*Merci infiniment!*
As meeting you I'm *enchanté.*
*Rien. Je ne regrette rien.*
O dramatic *Français!*

200

Sing my Barbara of Nantes,
Tell of your vagabond father
Who dies the night before your smile
Without farewell or 'I love you'
*Sans un adieu, sans un 'je t'aime'.*
O dolorous *Français!*

No slurring. In those speech organs
Such chic and naughty *savoir faire.*
Loveliest tongue. *La plus belle langue,*
Every sound seems to kiss a nerve,
Each word a bird of paradise.
O sensuous *Français!*


### 3

A hug as trains approached *un cadeau du ciel,*
Heaven sent. How could she have known at all?
*Merci infiniment!* Farewell.
Then two days later her unexpected call.
Assigned to Paris, wife in Poitiers,
Of course returning late and tired was rash,
She didn't want to shock but had to say
Her younger son had died in a motor crash.
Any common sense cries out against this fate.
'And all the same I trust.' *Quand même
Je crois en Dieu.* Unbreakable belief.
Was Job so tested – daughter, son and mate?
*Sans un adieu, sans un 'je t'aime'.*
Our time *à deux* an interlude in grief.

# Echo

Into my fifties when I began –
Too late for parent now or lover,
This time around brother or daughter.

First friend Shimizu-san 'Spring Water'
Babytalking me to discover
In myself some *déjà vu* Japan.

Other brothers too but often young
Women daughtering an older man,
Nurturing some new Japanese me.

'Peach-Tail' and 'High-up Mulberry Tree',
Momō-san and Takakuwa-san
Suckle me into another tongue.

Nakamura-san sighing *yoisho*
Or *yokkoisho* as she bent and swung
On her chair to lift a dictionary,

Sound of exertion 'ups-a-daisy',
A straining creak of an effort wrung
Out of the body, a 'yo-heave-ho'.

*Yoisho* I echo and have begun
As in second childhood to let go.
Brothers and daughters now cradle me.

A tongue-tied me now at last set free.
Dream I'd given up on years ago.
Words take wing into the rising sun.

## So

In the beginning
The word. So too in the end.
Birds of paradise.

Micheal O'Siadhail was born in 1947. He was educated at Clongowes Wood College, Trinity College Dublin, and the University of Oslo. A full-time writer, he has published twelve collections of poetry. He was awarded an Irish American Cultural Institute prize for poetry in 1982, and the Marten Toonder Prize for Literature in 1998. His poem suites, *The Naked Flame*, *Summerfest*, *Crosslight* and *Dublin Spring* were commissioned and set to music for performance and broadcasting.

His latest collections are *Our Double Time* (1998), *The Gossamer Wall: poems in witness to the Holocaust* (2002), *Love Life* (2005), *Globe* (2007) and *Tongues* (2010), all published by Bloodaxe. *Hail! Madam Jazz: New and Selected Poems* (Bloodaxe Books, 1992) included selections from five of his early collections, *The Leap Year* (1978), *Rungs of Time* (1980), *Belonging* (1982), *Springnight* (1983) and *The Image Wheel* (1985), as well as the whole of *The Chosen Garden* (1990) and a new collection, *The Middle Voice* (1992). *Poems 1975-1995*, drawing on both *Hail! Madam Jazz* and his later collection *A Fragile City* (1995), was published by Bloodaxe in 1999.

He has given poetry readings and broadcast extensively in Ireland, Britain, Europe, North America and Japan. In 1985 he was invited to give the Vernam Hull Lecture at Harvard and the Trumbull Lecture at Yale University. He represented Ireland at the Poetry Society's European Poetry Festival in London in 1981. He was writer-in-residence at the Yeats Summer School in 1991 and read at the Frankfurt Bookfair in 1997.

He has been a lecturer at Trinity College Dublin and a professor at the Dublin Institute for Advanced Studies. Among his many academic works are *Learning Irish* (Yale University Press, 1988) and *Modern Irish* (Cambridge University Press, 1989). He was a member of the Arts Council of the Republic of Ireland (1988-93) and of the Advisory Committee on Cultural Relations (1989-97), a founder member of Aosdána (Academy of distinguished Irish artists) and a former editor of *Poetry Ireland Review*. He is the founding chairman of ILE (Ireland Literature Exchange), and was a judge for *The Irish Times* ESB 1998 Theatre Awards and the 1998 *Sunday Tribune*/Hennessy Cognac Literary Awards.

*Micheal O'Siadhail's website:* www.osiadhail.com